C.M.N. ROGERS

Unbroken

First published by House of Nine Press 2025

Copyright © 2025 by C.M.N. ROGERS

All rights reserved. No part of this publication may be reproduced, stored or transmitted in any form or by any means, electronic, mechanical, photocopying, recording, scanning, or otherwise without written permission from the publisher. It is illegal to copy this book, post it to a website, or distribute it by any other means without permission.

C.M.N. ROGERS asserts the moral right to be identified as the author of this work.

First edition

ISBN: 978-1-7641620-4-3

This book was professionally typeset on Reedsy. Find out more at reedsy.com

*For the fallen, the fighting, and the finally free.
For my son and grandsons, the light that pulled me out.
And for every woman who needs to know she is stronger than the man who hurt her.*
OR
*To the ones who hid their bruises,
lied to protect the man who hurt them,
or cried in the shower so no one would hear.
To the women who stayed longer than they should have,
left later than they wanted to,
and blamed themselves long after it was over.*

Contents

Foreword iii
Content Warning iv
Disclaimer v
Author's Note on Structure & Flow vi
Prologue vii

I ORIGINS

Chapter 1 3
Reflection 10

II THE RELATIONSHIP

Chapter 1 15
Chapter 2 19
Reflection 25

III THE BREAKING POINT

Chapter 1 33
Chapter 2 38
Reflection 41

IV   THE AFTERMATH & HEALING

Chapter 1	51
Chapter 2	56
Chapter 3	59
Chapter 4	64
Chapter 5	68
Chapter 6	72
Chapter 7	78
Chapter 8	86
Chapter 9	93
Reflection	98

V   THRIVING

Chapter 1	105
Reflection	109

VI   TRUTH-BOMBS

Chapter 1	113
Chapter 2	118
Chapter 3	124
Chapter 4	127
Chapter 5	131
Author's Note About the Following Resources	137
Resources	139
A Compassionate Note for Survivors	141
About the Author	142
Also by C.M.N. ROGERS	143

Foreword

There are moments in life that fracture you so completely you wonder if you'll ever feel whole again. This book was born in the space between who I was, who I had to become to survive, and who I finally grew into when I chose myself.

I didn't write Unbroken to expose anyone. I wrote it to honour the women who never made it out, the women who are still silently surviving, and the women who are rebuilding their lives one breath at a time. I wrote it for my son and grandsons — the strongest reasons I had to keep fighting — and for the version of myself who walked through hell believing no one would ever understand. Some didn't. Some never will. But I am writing this for the ones who do.

This memoir is my truth. It is the story of how I lost myself, how I was shattered, and how I learned to rebuild a life I could finally recognise as my own. It's not a tidy story. Domestic violence never is. But I hope that in these pages, you find something that reminds you strength is not loud. Sometimes, strength is simply choosing to keep going.

If you are reading this as a survivor, you are not alone.

If you are reading this as a supporter, may it deepen your compassion.

And if you are reading this from inside a situation you cannot yet leave... may this book be a light in the darkest corners.

We heal by telling the truth — this is mine.

Content Warning

This book contains first-person accounts of domestic violence, including:
- emotional abuse
- physical assault
- strangulation
- sexual coercion
- trauma bonding
- psychological manipulation
- suicidal thoughts
- descriptions of injuries
- police intervention
- recovery after abuse

These sections are written with honesty and clarity to support survivors and shed light on the reality of domestic violence.

If at any point you feel overwhelmed, please pause, take a breath, and return when you feel ready.

Your wellbeing comes first.

If you are currently unsafe or in crisis, please contact your local emergency services or a domestic violence support hotline listed in the resource section of this book.

You are not alone.

Disclaimer

This memoir is a true account of my personal experiences. The events described in these pages reflect my memories, perceptions, and emotional reality during the time they occurred.

For privacy and safety, names and identifying details of individuals and locations have been changed. These changes do not alter the essence or truth of my story.

This book is not intended to target, accuse, or defame any individual. It is offered for the purposes of awareness, healing, and empowerment.

The reflections and insights in this book are based on my own lived experience and are not a substitute for professional medical, psychological, or legal advice. If you or someone you know is experiencing domestic violence, please seek assistance from qualified support services or emergency professionals.

Author's Note on Structure & Flow

Unbroken moves between two threads: the story of what happened, and the understanding I gained only years later.

The memoir unfolds chronologically — from childhood, to the relationship, to the breaking point, to the years of rebuilding. After each major section, I include short Reflection Chapters: insights, patterns, and psychological truths I didn't have at the time. These reflections are my hindsight — the meaning I made from the chaos, the clarity I found long after my body had already escaped.

I chose this structure intentionally.

Surviving domestic violence is not a straight line. It is a cycle.

Healing is not linear. It is a spiral.

Understanding comes in layers, arriving when we are finally safe enough to face it.

By telling the story first and the insight second, I hope to give readers:

the emotional immersion of walking through the moments with me, and

the grounded understanding that helps make sense of them.

This book is both testimony and guide.

It is the story of how I broke, how I rebuilt, and how I finally rose into the woman I am today.

Prologue

There are moments you don't speak of for years — not because you're afraid of them, but because you don't yet have the language to describe the way they lived inside your body.

Mine carried the truth long before my mind was ready to face it.

A slammed door made my pulse spike.

A sudden shift in tone tightened my breath.

A shadow in my peripheral vision could send a cold sweep across my chest.

But nothing showed on the outside.

I didn't shake.

I didn't cry.

I didn't fall apart.

I smiled.

I laughed at jokes.

I brightened my voice when people asked how I was.

I performed "I'm fine" with a level of skill that should have earned awards.

Masking became muscle-memory — a polished version of myself I could slip into no matter what bruises hid beneath my clothes or what fear sat lodged beneath my ribs.

And then came the morning — the quiet one — when I finally looked at myself in the mirror and saw what the mask had been hiding.

Not the injuries.

Not the swelling.

Not the marks I'd grown so used to covering.
It was the look in my own eyes.
A hollowness.
A fatigue so deep it felt ancient.
A woman standing before me who looked like she was slowly fading out of her own life.
I didn't recognise her.
And in that stillness — that clarity — I realised something devastating:
I wasn't just being hurt.
I was losing myself.
That was the turning point.
Not the first assault.
Not the arguments I smoothed over.
Not the nights I went to bed pretending everything was normal.
It was the morning my reflection stopped lying for me.
Because you can endure almost anything while you can still tell yourself a story that makes it bearable.
You can rationalise.
You can minimise.
You can survive.
But when you finally see the truth in your own eyes, something inside you refuses to keep living the same way.
My body had known long before my mind did.
My reflection forced me to listen.
This memoir does not begin with the violence that nearly killed me.
It begins with the moment I realised I had drifted so far from myself — and the moment I decided I wouldn't keep slipping away.
It is a story of leaving, yes — but more importantly, it is a story of returning.
Returning to myself.
Returning to my worth.

Returning to the woman I was always meant to be.

And if you are reading this quietly, secretly, hiding behind your own smile, I want you to know something from the very first page:

Your mask is not your truth.

Your body already knows.

And you are allowed to choose yourself.

This is where my story begins.

With the decision to rise.

I

ORIGINS

1

ORIGINS

Chapter 1

*"Every beginning leaves marks —
but it also leaves clues for who we become."*

I didn't grow up in a gentle world.

Violence was the background noise of my childhood — sometimes loud, sometimes whispered, but always there, shaping me long before I had the language to understand it.

My father was addicted to heroin, and the addiction consumed him until there was nothing left but lies, fists, and the kind of disorder children learn to navigate by instinct alone. He disappeared emotionally long before he disappeared physically.

The last night he lived in our home is burned into me. Mum had locked him out after he brought his girlfriend home — bold, brazen, a man who treated betrayal as habit. He smashed through the door. I shoved my little brother into the hallway cupboard and ran for the phone, but the girlfriend ripped it from my hands and hit me. I bolted behind the couch while the house erupted. Dad hit Mum. Mum climbed onto the couch — she's tiny — and smashed him across the head with a frying pan until blood hit the walls.

When they finally left, I followed her down the hallway to the bathroom.

"Are you okay?" I asked.

"Better than that bastard will feel tomorrow," she said, and carried on like nothing had happened.

He never came home again. I was around seven.

To most people, the absence of a violent man should be a relief. But children don't understand the adult logic of harm and safety. They only understand longing — the ache of not being chosen.

It bothered me deeply that he never wanted to see my brother or me.

Mum told us he didn't want children — not then, not really ever. Maybe later, she said. Maybe when we were older, as though love could be scheduled like an appointment.

But I internalised something else entirely:

That I was forgettable.

That I was unimportant.

That I was unlovable.

That even my own father found me disposable.

And when a girl grows up believing she can be discarded, it becomes far too easy to accept crumbs later and call it love.

The world outside wasn't gentler.

I grew up in a rough part of Auckland, surrounded by aggression that mirrored home. Fights in the street. Shouting behind thin walls. Kids who knew too much. Adults who didn't care enough. You learn fast in an environment like that: keep your head down, use your fists when you need to, and take things in stride because that's what everyone else is doing.

And then, at eight years old, a different kind of violence found me.

The kind that doesn't leave bruises you can point to, the kind you don't have words for at that age, the kind adults rarely notice because they're too wrapped up in their own lives.

It began with an older cousin.

A trusted face.

A closed door.

CHAPTER 1

The first time wasn't in a dark bedroom or in some foreboding alleyway — it was in the toilet block at the golf course we walked through after school. That's how ordinary it was. I didn't sense danger; he was my cousin.

But that's how predators work — they use trust like a key.

I worked out what was happening quickly enough, to ensure my compliance he welded the fear of God into me: "If you tell anyone, I'll burn your brother alive." My brother was two years younger. I adored him. That threat silenced me for five years.

I swallowed the fear.

I swallowed the truth.

By thirteen, secrecy was second nature.

I wore a mask without knowing I'd put one on. I had learned — without anyone saying a word — that my body wasn't mine to protect, and that other people's wants could eclipse my right to safety.

When my stepfather entered the picture around the same time, people thought our family finally looked "normal." He was older, confident, put-together. From the outside, we looked like a blended family that had stabilised after danger.

Behind closed doors was a different story.

He was fiery, controlling, easily angered, and full of opinions about children who weren't his. In his world, we were to be seen and not heard. The smallest things could set him off — a tone of voice, a misplaced object, a pair of shoes he hated.

I remember those shoes.

I loved them. I'd bought them myself.

He cut them up in front of me.

A simple act but a devastating message:

Who you are is unacceptable.

What you love can be destroyed.

His anger didn't have tells. He could be laughing one minute and throwing something across the yard the next. It wasn't calculated cruelty, not in the way I'd later experience as an adult — it was old-school, dominant, my-way-or-the-highway shit. And because he and Mum loved each other fiercely, that volatility was protected, minimised, justified. Their bond was impenetrable — and my brother and I learned quickly that we lived outside their circle.

And so, I learned another lesson:

That love was conditional.

That safety was conditional.

That approval could be withdrawn at any moment.

Our house was permanent eggshells. My bedroom became my sanctuary — a small world where I could hide with a book, my sewing machine, or my knitting for hours. That was the first place I learned that solitude felt safer than people.

These were the foundations of my childhood — addiction, violence, silence, exclusion, and the constant sense that my needs, my voice, my worth were secondary to maintaining peace.

I didn't realise it then, but those years were teaching me how to tolerate anything.

How to normalise harm.

How to swallow pain.

How to stay even when everything in me wanted to run.

I grew up believing that to receive love, I had to endure whatever came with it.

That bad behaviour was the price of belonging.

That being hurt was simply part of being wanted.

These early years didn't just shape me —

they carved the blueprint for every relationship that followed.

By the time I reached my early teens, the pressure inside me had nowhere left to go. Years of being silenced, controlled, overlooked, and violated had built up like steam in a sealed container. I became an angry

CHAPTER 1

teenager — defensive, quick to ignite, sharp-edged in every direction. Not because I was bad, but because rage was the only language I had left.

Anger became a comfortable pair of shoes—well-worn, reliable, easy to step into. Inside, it felt like a banked fire waiting for the smallest spark. I scared myself sometimes. I scared other people too. I learned early that when I lost my shit, I could burn someone down emotionally, verbally, energetically.

Years later, when my brother found out I'd been in a DV relationship, he said, "Fuck mate, why didn't you bury the c*nt in the backyard? You would have a few years ago."

He wasn't wrong.

One day, after yet another clash with my stepfather, something in me snapped. I packed a bag and walked out. No fear. No hesitation. No plan. Just done.

Leaving home young wasn't brave.

It was survival.

I went to live with my father's parents. Their home wasn't perfect, but it was safe in the ways I desperately needed — predictable where my childhood home was not. For the first time, the world around me stopped vibrating with someone else's anger.

But the anger inside me didn't vanish.

It lived under my skin, ready to flare, because that's what happens when pain has nowhere else to go. I had learned to fight with my fists when the world demanded it. I had learned to shout when no one listened. I had learned to defend myself with the only tools my childhood had given me.

Before I left home, a boy moved in next door. I was fourteen and he disarmed me completely.

My son's father.

He was calm where I was fiery, gentle where I was hardened, patient where I was impulsive. We didn't start dating until I was seventeen — life took its turns in the years between — but even from the beginning, I recognised something in him:

Safety.

He was my first voluntary relationship — the first time I chose to be close to someone who wasn't dangerous, controlling, or explosive. And I didn't know how to receive that kind of steady affection, not at first. Unpredictability had been my normal for so long that calm felt suspicious.

But he stayed steady.

He didn't push.

He didn't demand.

We moved in together when I was seventeen, and for fifteen years we built a life. It wasn't perfect — no long relationship is — but it was not violent, manipulative or coercive. He was, and still is, a good man. A gentle man. A soul who anchored me in ways I didn't know I needed.

It was with him that I first learned what it felt like to walk through a doorway without bracing.

To sleep without fear.

To explore who I was without someone else shaping me through their anger.

He helped carve out the first pocket of peace I had ever known.

But peace does not heal old wounds by itself.

It simply gives them space to rise.

All those buried patterns — the abandonment, the silence, the conditional love, the learned tolerance of harm — stayed dormant, waiting for a moment years later when someone would trigger every old hurt I thought I had outrun.

The truth is this:

I didn't form a sense of self-worth in my teenage years.

I simply found a place to rest.

CHAPTER 1

Healing came much later — after the relationship that nearly cost me my life.

But the roots were planted here:

in a childhood that taught me to endure anything,

and a teenage rebellion that taught me I could leave when staying became unbearable.

Reflection

*"Reflection is where pain becomes clarity —
and clarity becomes freedom."*

Childhood → patterns → how self-worth formed

When I look back on my childhood, I don't see isolated events.

I see a pattern — a slow shaping — a long conditioning that taught me who I was allowed to be in the world. Those years weren't just memories; they were instructions. They laid the groundwork for how I understood love, safety, and my own worth.

Growing up in violence taught me that people could love you and hurt you in the same breath.

It taught me that the adults meant to protect you can also be the ones you fear.

It taught me that yelling was normal, that silence was safer, and that walking on eggshells was a daily rhythm.

When that is your first language, you grow up fluent in danger — and unable to recognise safety for what it is.

I didn't know it then, but I had been conditioned — quietly, consistently — to normalise the unacceptable:

to minimise pain,

to stay quiet to keep the peace,

to fight when pushed,

to tolerate harm as the price of belonging.

Each person in my childhood played a part in that training:

My father taught me that love could vanish overnight, and abandonment was something to expect.

My cousin taught me that my body could be stolen from me, and silence was the cost of protecting others.

My stepfather taught me that who I was could be punished, and approval revoked without warning.

My mother's choices taught me that my safety was negotiable, and that I wasn't someone worth defending.

These are not small lessons.

They become the architecture of adulthood.

By the time I reached my twenties, my nervous system had been built for survival, not connection. I anticipated impact, not affection. I understood anger more easily than patience. And because I had spent my entire childhood managing other people's moods, I learned two things extremely well:

- how to keep the peace
- and how to explode when pushed too far.

Both followed me into adult relationships.

It wasn't that I didn't want love.

It was that I didn't believe I had the right to ask for it without paying a price.

So, when kindness appeared, I didn't trust it.

When someone treated me gently, I didn't know how to receive it.

And when calm finally entered my life, it felt unfamiliar.

Which is why, years later, when I met someone whose behaviour echoed the shadows of my childhood, my body recognised the rhythm long before my mind understood it.

Trauma doesn't just leave wounds; it leaves patterns.

We gravitate toward what we know, even when what we know has harmed us.

I didn't choose the relationship that nearly destroyed me because I was weak, naïve, or unaware.

I chose it because it matched the blueprint I had been trained to survive:

instability, emotional swings, conditional affection.

It felt, on a nervous-system level, like "home" — not safe, but familiar.

Survival wasn't new to me.

It was the foundation I had been raised on.

And yet, inside the girl who endured so much, there was also a spark —

the same spark that hid her brother in a cupboard,

the same spark that walked out of her childhood home,

the same spark that, years later, would walk away from a man who mirrored every old wound.

This is where understanding begins.

This is where the past stops being a story and becomes a map — a map that explains how a child raised in the wreckage of other people's damage becomes a woman who tolerates far too much in the name of love.

This reflection is not an excuse.

It is a compassionate explanation.

Because healing doesn't begin with blaming yourself for what you didn't know.

It begins with understanding how you learned to navigate a world that never taught you safety.

Now we can turn the page —

to the relationship that reflected my past so precisely

it nearly swallowed my future.

II

THE RELATIONSHIP

II

THE RELATIONSHIP

Chapter 1

*"A wolf doesn't need to snarl to be dangerous —
sometimes it only needs to smile."*

We met online, the way people do when they've both lived long enough to doubt fairytales but still quietly hope for one. He was FIFO, I was overseas, and for four straight weeks we talked every day — long messages, late-night calls, the kind of rapid, intense connection that makes you think the universe is finally giving you something back.

I didn't know then that he was having the same conversations with half a dozen other women.

All I knew was that he made me feel wanted.

By the time we finally met for a quick drink at a local pub, I felt like I already knew him. I remember walking toward him and feeling something I brushed off as nerves — a flicker in my gut I ignored because I hadn't dated in years and assumed I was simply rusty.

He was charming. Intelligent. Funny. Attentive. Attractive.

The kind of man who could fill a room.

Looking back, I can see the performance in it.

But at the time, I felt special.

He swept me quickly into his world — road trips, motorbikes, kayaking, camping by rivers deep in the bush. We both loved dogs, which felt like a sign. I hadn't expected to meet someone who wanted adventure at my pace, someone who seemed to match me stride for stride.

For the first time in years, I began to imagine a future with someone. Marriage. Growing old together.

But there were small fractures early on — tiny things I dismissed.

One day he organised lunch. I waited, then hours past the allotted time, messaged him, and eventually got a distracted:

"Sorry babe, I forgot — I'm at my mate's. We can do dinner instead."

Another time we were out, and his friend — in front of both of us — said,

"Mate, if you want to keep her, maybe stop checking out every woman who walks past."

I laughed it off, pretending it didn't bother me. Of course it did.

I told myself men take longer to attach.

I gave him time.

The lies started small too — little inconsistencies, small edits of the truth.

I called them out.

He hated that.

There was also the drinking. Heavy. Habitual. When he tried cutting back, his mood swung so quickly it felt like walking through a minefield.

And then there was his ex.

He told me they still lived together because of finances — FIFO schedule, shared house, legal agreements. He even showed me documents. Because I'd had such a calm co-parenting relationship with my son's father, the arrangement didn't strike me as strange.

But months passed.

And he still wouldn't let me come to the house.

He'd turn up at mine distressed, angry, emotional, talking about arguments with her.

It didn't feel like the beginning of something new.

CHAPTER 1

It felt tangled and messy.
Eventually I said what anyone would say:
"If you want a relationship with me, she needs to move out."
He resisted.
Then did it.
And then for years in his rages he blamed me — telling me I'd forced his hand, that he hadn't been ready.
That was the first real crack.
Around the same time, I found a text arranging a visit to a prostitute.
When I confronted him, he looked at me with a coldness I will never forget and said:
"She's just a hooker. Who cares? Get over it."
I cared.
Of course I cared.
And I left.
He texted all night — apologies, declarations, promises, panic.
I ignored him.
By morning he said he needed to "make things right," that he was desperate, terrified, remorseful.
I felt torn — angry, hurt, confused — but compassion won, as it always had in my life.
I relented.
I went to his house.
I walked through the garage expecting a conversation, maybe a final attempt at repair.
Instead, he shut the door, dragged me inside, and shoved me across the space.
The shock was instant. Disbelief collided with one thought: *What the fuck is happening?*
He kept yelling — accusations that made no sense. When the handlebar of his pushbike slammed into my stomach, knocking the air

out of me, I finally realised I was in real danger.

I tried to calm him, to talk him down — the way I'd been trained to respond to anger my whole life. I told him I would leave and we could talk later. But he stood between me and the only exit.

Panic and confusion skittered through me.

This was a man I had trusted.

A man I had imagined a future with.

That was the first act of violence.

Not the worst — but the one that split the ground beneath my feet and dropped me into a world I didn't yet know I was trapped inside.

And after the sobbing, the apologies, the promises, the shaking remorse...

I forgave him.

But something fundamental in me snapped that day.

My trust was gone — and it never came back.

Much later I would come to understand that by going back after this incident gave him permission to treat me any way he damn well chose.

And so the cycle began.

Chapter 2

*"Not every prison has bars —
some are built from promises and hope."*

After the day in the garage, the cycle began in full force.

The violence was always followed by remorse so dramatic and convincing it felt like a different man had replaced the one who shoved me into his bike. The apologies were cinematic — tears, trembling hands, broken voice, stories of trauma, declarations that he was damaged, terrified of abandonment, desperate to be better.

He would curl around me like a child and whisper:

"I'm sorry, my beautiful little Carols."

"I only go crazy because I love you so much."

"I have abandonment issues because I'm adopted."

"It's all my fault. I'll fix myself."

"I'll go to therapy."

"I'll be the man you deserve."

He said these things with such frantic sincerity that some part of me — the part trained since childhood to soothe angry people — wanted to believe him.

And every time, I forgave him.

Every single time.

Even when my lips were split.

Even when my face and body was bruised.

Even when there were strangulation marks around my neck.

In the beginning, the "honeymoon" stage lasted weeks. Then days. Then hours. Eventually, there was almost no calm between storms — just brief moments where he became the man I fell for long enough to reset my hope before tearing everything down again.

He didn't just apologise.

He made grand gestures.

Like the ring.

A beautiful amethyst set in silver. He handed it to me and told me it was a commitment ring — a promise that one day, when he "fixed himself," he would marry me.

"You're the love of my life," he said.

"I just need time to become the man you deserve."

It hooked me so deeply that even now I can feel the ache of it — the way hope can blind you long after you should have walked away.

But the violence escalated the way it always does: slowly, then all at once.

He would throw me to the floor.

Restrain me.

Spit in my face.

Headbutt me until I saw stars.

Smash my head against the floorboards.

Strangle me.

Punch me between my legs while screaming obscenities.

Twice, he tried to run me off the road.

There was a moment I will never forget — the knife.

He brought it down, aiming for my head, and God knows how, but I dodged and the bloody thing got stuck in the mattress. That split second of resistance gave me just enough time to scramble away. It wasn't strength that saved me. It wasn't courage.

CHAPTER 2

It was luck.

Stupid, blind luck.

Then came the hot coffee — thrown deliberately onto my genitals, because I had asked for some time out after a brutal assault.

And the worst part was the look on his face whenever he hurt me.

Every time he lost his shit, his whole expression shifted — the smirk, the way his normally blue eyes went black, the flicker of pleasure he took in watching me crumble.

His entire face changed.

And I swear to Christ... he enjoyed it.

It was written all over him.

He even told me there was something wrong with him because he got turned on when I started fighting back. So, he'd provoke me — slap me upside the head, jab me in the face — anything to push me until I reacted.

And while all that was happening, the cheating just escalated. Every assault seemed to coincide with a fresh betrayal: messages to other women, emails to prostitutes, secret meet-ups. And when I confronted him, he would call me crazy and deny everything.

Once, when I found another woman's dirty underwear in the drawer I used to use at his house, he shoved them into my mouth — a humiliation I didn't even understand until later, when I learned he'd cheated the night before.

He would rage at me, physically assault me, drive me away — then go out and do the very thing he accused me of imagining.

Then, like clockwork, the messages would come:

"Please don't leave me."

"You're the only one I've ever truly loved."

"I'll change."

And I went back.

Not because I was weak — but because my nervous system had been trained since childhood to confuse instability with connection, intensity with love.

Along the way, he added a new line:

"If you just did as you were told and didn't ask so many questions, I wouldn't have to hit you."

And somewhere inside me — in the place shaped by abandonment, violation, and conditional love — that sentence found fertile ground.

My life began collapsing around me in small, almost unnoticeable ways.

I started comfort eating.

Chips, chocolate, ice cream, takeaway — anything to numb the constant anxiety. I gained weight quickly, the opposite of the healthy lifestyle I had always lived. Before him, I juiced daily, grew my own vegetables, owned gyms, ate well, cared for myself. With him, I barely recognised the person in the mirror.

I stopped my hobbies.

I stopped sleeping.

My body was always on alert.

If I tried knitting in bed at night — something that once soothed me — he would ridicule me. If I brought out my laptop to write or design while he slept, he would complain, saying he wanted to cuddle and couldn't because I was "always doing something."

I became adept at hiding bruises, using makeup as armour. My daughter-in-law quietly told my son she suspected he was hitting me long before I admitted it.

Then came the cancer.

I was diagnosed with endometrial cancer and had major surgery — frightening, invasive, emotionally overwhelming. Most people imagine a partner stepping up during something like that.

He didn't.

He kicked and punched me in the stomach while I was still healing.

CHAPTER 2

He told me he wanted me to bleed out on his floor.

He meant it.

I could see it in his eyes.

The police got involved the night I drove myself to the hospital dizzy and vomiting. One of his headbutts had caused a concussion. I walked into emergency trying to hide the truth. The nurses didn't buy a word of it. They saw everything I was trying to conceal. They put me into a room on my own, then called the police and a social worker, and that's how I ended up in the high-risk DV team.

He went to jail — twice.

Once for injuring me.

The second time for breaching the DVO when the neighbours called the police because he was screaming at me.

And yet he convinced half his world I was unstable.

Even after admitting what he'd done, his friends defended him.

They still do.

During those years, my behaviour looked erratic from the outside.

Of course it did.

I was living in a war zone that no one else could see.

I lied to my family, my friends, everyone. Not to protect him, but to protect myself from shame and the inevitable question:

"Why don't you just leave?"

They didn't know I had tried.

Many times.

They didn't know leaving a violent man isn't a simple decision — it's a strategy, a calculation, a timing issue. One wrong move can cost you everything, including your life.

He never controlled me financially, but he used money as punishment. Sometimes he beat me until I returned gifts he had bought me. One Christmas, after an argument, he headbutted me repeatedly until I transferred $400 to his account to "repay" the gift he had given me.

When the money didn't clear instantly — weekend banking delay — he hit me again.
I lived my life shrinking.
Explaining.
Appeasing.
Absorbing.
Forgiving.
Pretending.
Reacting.
There were dozens of moments that should have been the point of no return.
But each time, the cycle pulled me back in.
Because the apologies were intoxicating.
Because the love bombing was powerful.
Because the cycle was all-consuming.
Because I believed, against all evidence, that he could become the man he kept promising to be.
And because denial is a fortress — and I lived inside it.
It wasn't until the caravan — that night of headbutts, screaming, and humiliation in front of strangers — that something inside me finally broke.
Not my body.
My denial.
That was the night I knew with absolute clarity:
If I didn't leave, I would die.
And that clarity is why I am here writing this — because so many women never get to that moment.

Reflection

"The most dangerous place in a violent relationship is the hope that he might change."

The Psychology of the Trap

People on the outside always ask the same question, with the same bewildered tone:

"Why didn't you just leave?"

I used to ask myself that too.

But the truth is:

I didn't stay because I didn't know the difference between right and wrong.

I didn't stay because I enjoyed the drama or craved the pain.

I stayed because I had been conditioned since childhood to absorb harm from the people I loved, and because he weaponised every crack in me with precision.

I only learned that truth later, when healing forced me to look backward and see the patterns that had been shaping me my whole life.

He knew exactly which version of himself to give me.

There was the charming man — the one who took me on adventures, who looked at me like I was the answer to a question he'd been asking his whole life.

There was the vulnerable boy — the one who cried in my arms, shaking, telling me he didn't want to lose me, that he was broken inside, that no one had ever loved him the way I did.

And then there was the monster — the one who hurt me, humiliated me, and blamed me for the violence he unleashed.

People don't understand how violent men operate.

They don't start with the monster.

They start with the love story.

And when the monster eventually appears, the woman already has a hundred memories of the man she fell for — memories that convince her he's still in there somewhere, if she just loves him enough.

My empathy was a trap he counted on.

I'm a naturally compassionate person.

I forgive easily.

I understand too much.

I make excuses for people based on what they've survived.

He saw all of that in me — and he exploited it.

Every time he cried, every time he curled into me like a terrified child, every time he promised he'd change, something inside me softened.

He knew it would.

He played the victim so well he should have been on the stage.

He spoke in therapy phrases — broken, trauma, abandonment issues, "you're the only one who sees me," "I'm trying so hard."

And because I believe in growth — because I have grown from my past — I believed he could too.

When in fact he never intended to.

This is the part people don't want to hear:

When you grow up in violence, you learn to see it as normal.

Not acceptable.

Not desirable.

Just... familiar.

I didn't bat an eyelash at yelling.

REFLECTION

I didn't shy away from anger.
I didn't interpret a raised voice as danger.
I had lived through far worse in childhood.
So when he shoved me, screamed at me, threw me around — my brain didn't scream run.
It screamed manage it.
Calm him.
Fix it.
That conditioning is powerful.
It takes root before you're even old enough to understand what's being done to you.
And then there was the trauma bond.
I didn't know what that was at the time.
I didn't have a social worker or a therapist explaining it to me — there was no one because the system was overwhelmed.
So, I learned from living inside it.
A trauma bond is a psychological leash built out of:
affection
abuse
fear
guilt
intermittent reinforcement
It's the same cycle casinos use to keep you pulling the lever.
You get just enough love to stay.
Just enough remorse to forgive.
Just enough fantasy to hope.
Just enough terror to keep you compliant.
By the time I realised what was happening, I wasn't just attached to him — I was chemically hooked.
Dopamine.
Adrenaline.

Cortisol.

The whole cocktail.

My nervous system thought he was safety — simply because he wasn't hurting me in that moment.

That's what people don't get:

Your body bonds to your abuser in the same way it bonds to a caregiver.

It's biological cruelty.

But the biggest lie I told myself was the most dangerous one.

I didn't believe he would kill me.

I truly didn't.

I convinced myself I would always survive him.

I even joked about it once during a calm moment.

He laughed and said,

"Don't be stupid, I'd never kill you. But if I did, I'd wrap you in carpet and chicken wire and dump you in the lake so no one would find you."

I laughed along with him.

That's how deep the trap was.

People think strong women don't end up in relationships like this.

Bullshit.

Strong women survive domestic violence because of their strength — not because they lack it.

Strong women:

endure more

rationalise more

grit their teeth longer

carry hope like a weapon

believe they can fix things

believe in people

forgive too much

absorb too much

REFLECTION

silence themselves to keep the peace
get hooked harder because they love harder
Strong women don't leave quickly.
They leave when they see death.
And even then, it takes everything.

***

The internal conflict tore me apart.
I had hope.
I had fear.
I had the fantasy.
I had the reality.
I had the charming man in my head.
I had the monster in front of me.
I had the tough version of myself.
I had the broken version he created.
All of them lived inside me at once.
And that's what made the bond so hard to break.
This is the truth women rarely tell in DV memoirs — not because they're hiding it, but because it's hard to articulate:
You fall in love with the man he pretends to be.
You survive the man he really is.
And you stay because the space between those two versions becomes its own kind of prison.
And this chapter — this reflection — is the bridge.
Because the next chapter is the caravan.
The breaking point.
The clarity.
The moment I finally, finally saw the truth:
If I didn't leave, death was a foregone conclusion.

III

THE BREAKING POINT

Chapter 1

*"The moment you ignore your intuition
is the moment danger finds its opening."*

It was supposed to be a romantic getaway.
His idea.
His promise.
A "reset," he called it — the chance to fix what had been breaking for years.
Even as we packed the caravan, something in me twisted.
A warning.
My intuition had been whispering for days, but by the time we pulled onto the highway, it was screaming.
I told him I felt off.
He told me I was being silly.
And I wanted to believe him.

***

The Setup
Earlier in the day, he'd asked if I wanted to be intimate later — said it with that soft, sweet tone he used when he was baiting a future fight. Intimacy was rare between us. Always promised, rarely delivered.
But I still said yes.
Of course I did.

I was starving for connection — emotional, physical, any kind of closeness that didn't come with an apology attached.

After our showers that night, I knew instantly he had no intention of following through.

His body language changed.

His voice went flat.

Suddenly he was "really tired," "headache," "done for the night."

The script was familiar.

I went quiet.

Not sulking.

Not angry.

Just... quiet.

The kind of quiet women use when they know speaking comes with a fist.

"Babe, what's wrong?"

"Talk to me."

"Come on, it's safe to tell me the truth."

He pushed.

And pushed.

And pushed.

Until silence wasn't an option anymore.

"I'm just disappointed," I said softly. "You said we could be close tonight. But it's okay."

And that was it.

That single sentence.

A spark on dry tinder.

He exploded so fast the air changed.

One second he was sitting.

The next he was towering over me — voice raised, face twisted, yelling words so loud they shook the thin walls of the caravan.

Obscenities.

CHAPTER 1

Accusations.

Venom thrown at point-blank range.

I was on the bed, leaning toward the TV, trying to fix the signal, and then his hands were on me — grabbing, dragging, shoving.

The mattress slammed against my spine.

The air left my lungs in a rush.

His forehead cracked against mine once—

twice—

a third time.

Pain burst behind my eyes.

I remember thinking, *What the fuck is happening?*

And just as quickly: *How do I get out? Where is the door? How do I get past him?*

He spat in my face.

I kept my voice low, trying to calm him.

Telling him to stop.

Telling him he was hurting me.

Begging him to breathe.

He didn't hear a word.

Or maybe he did — and that's what fuelled him.

When he finally lurched back, high on adrenaline, I looked out the caravan window and saw silhouettes turning toward us.

Other campers.

Other couples.

Families.

No one came over.

No one intervened.

But honestly, I didn't want them to.

He was so dangerous in that state that I would rather be the one hurt than see a stranger step into the line of fire.

The whole showground felt surreal —

soft chatter in the distance, laughter drifting through the dark, the glow of campfires, the clink of cutlery on enamel plates.

Normal life happening metres away from my nightmare.

I don't remember the moment my body decided to move.

Only the sensation of cold air hitting my face as I bolted out of the caravan.

Then darkness.

A wide-open paddock.

Crickets buzzing.

My heart pounding so loud it drowned out everything else.

I ran until my lungs told me to quit.

Until I couldn't see the lights anymore.

Until I felt hidden.

I stayed there for over an hour — crouched low, shaking, crying, furious and sick with the realisation that I was in actual danger again, and I had no one else to blame but myself.

He didn't look for me.

Instead, he packed up.

The metallic clatter of the caravan hitch, the rustle of gear being thrown inside — I heard it from across the dark.

And that's when it hit me:

He's going to leave.

He's going to drive away.

And everything I own is in that van.

My phone.

My money.

My clothes.

My entire means of escape.

The trapped feeling spread through me like ice water.

I knew I had no choice.

I had to go back.

CHAPTER 1

Walking toward that caravan was one of the hardest things I've ever done.

Each step felt like walking back into a burning building for something essential you can't live without.

When I climbed in, we didn't speak.

He drove in silence — three and a half hours, headlights cutting through the night, the steering wheel gripped in his hands like he was wishing it was my throat.

When we got to my place, past midnight, he refused to take me to my truck.

I told him to sleep in the caravan.

He refused that too.

Instead, he came inside with me, switching instantly into the familiar post-violence softness — apologies, affection, the performance of remorse so well-rehearsed it almost felt believable.

I kept the peace.

Because I had a plan.

Chapter 2

"Leaving doesn't begin with a door.
It begins with a decision."

It was still dark outside when he woke up and told me to get up.

My head throbbed when I sat upright, a pounding reminder of the night before.

"Get up. We're going," he was irritated.

I rose immediately.

Not because I was afraid of him in that moment, but because my mind was already focused on one thing:

Get my truck.

Get away.

Do not give him a reason to spark again.

I wasn't trying to soothe him the way I used to.

I was steady.

Quiet.

Resolved.

Something inside me had settled during the long, silent drive home the night before — a deep knowing that whatever I had been holding onto was gone.

And he could feel it.

There wasn't much conversation.

CHAPTER 2

Not in the house.

Not in the car.

Not as the sky slowly lightened around us.

He was angry, but not explosive — more annoyed, inconvenienced, fed up.

He blamed me for "ruining the trip," as though a promise he broke and violence he initiated were inconveniences I had created.

I didn't respond.

There was nothing left to say.

We drove to his place in silence.

It was a silence without tension this time — more like two people who had reached the same conclusion from opposite directions:

This is done.

When we pulled into his driveway, he didn't ask how I was.

He didn't reflect on what happened.

He didn't show remorse.

Instead, he asked me to help with a few things — small, practical tasks.

And I did them, quietly, deliberately, because keeping the peace was the last step in getting out cleanly.

He seemed just as ready for the end as I was.

Not devastated.

Not clinging.

Almost relieved.

And that was when I realised:

I had never been his partner.

I had been his outlet.

His possession.

His relief.

His entertainment.

His punching bag.

His audience.
Never his equal.
Never his priority.
Never someone he intended to treat with care.

When everything was finished, I walked to my truck — my own space, my own key, my own escape — and got in.

No goodbye.
No last words.
No final round of apologies or promises or theatrics.
Just closure in its starkest form.

As I drove away, something in me broke — not in the way trauma breaks you, but in the way truth breaks delusion.

I cried the entire drive home.
Not because I missed him.
Not because I wanted him back.
Not because I doubted myself.

But because I finally understood that the fantasy I had been clinging to — the version of him I wanted him to be, the future I thought we were building — was never real.

It was a story I'd written in my own mind, a story built on hope, scraps of affection, and promises that were always empty.

And on that morning, as the sun rose and the highway curved beneath my tyres, that story finally died.

I was done.
Truly, finally, irrevocably done.

And the woman driving that truck home was not the same woman who had climbed into the caravan two nights before.

She was resolute.
She was beginning — to come back to herself.

Reflection

"Rock bottom isn't an event — it's the moment your soul whispers, 'No more.'"

What a breaking point really looks like
People talk about "rock bottom" like it's a single, dramatic moment.
One event.
One punch.
One night.
But the truth is, you hit emotional rock bottom over and over again long before anyone sees you leave.
There were so many nights that should have been my breaking point.
The first time he shoved me in the garage.
The first time he spat in my face.
The first time he strangled me.
The first time I left his house black and blue.
The first time I drove myself to hospital with a concussion.
The first hooker I found out about.
Every one of those moments was enough.
Enough for any sane person.
Enough for any outsider looking in.
Enough to say: "That's it. I'm done."
But I didn't leave for good after those.

I'd like to say I don't know why.
But I do.
And if you've lived this, you do too.

***

Your Body Knows Before Your Mind Does

By the time I got to the caravan, my body was done long before my mind would admit it.

My gut clenching every time his phone rang.

My shoulders tightening when he changed tone.

My lungs holding air whenever he walked into a room until I could gauge his mood.

My body had been saying no for years.

But I kept saying yes with my behaviour.

Yes to one more chance.

Yes to one more apology.

Yes to one more "I'll change, I promise."

Yes to one more cycle I already knew the ending of.

What changed in the caravan wasn't that he suddenly became violent. He'd already done that. Repeatedly.

What changed was that everything collided at once:

the humiliation of being screamed at and headbutted in a public place

the realisation that not one person came to help (and that I didn't want them to, because I knew how dangerous he was)

the sick feeling of watching him pack up the van, knowing he would leave me there if I didn't go back

the split-second awareness that if he could do this here, he could do absolutely anything, anywhere.

My nervous system finally stopped bargaining.

It stopped negotiating.

It stopped trying to make him make sense.

It stopped trying to pretty up reality.

REFLECTION

That night, alone in the dark paddock with my heart hammering and my body shaking, there was no fantasy left to hide behind. No ring. No future. No "maybe this time." Just the bare, ugly truth:

He is capable of killing me.
And if I keep doing this, one day he will.
My body understood that first.
My mind took longer to catch up.

***

Why "The Worst" Moment Isn't Always the Last One

People think the most brutal assault is the one that makes you leave. It's almost comforting for them to believe that — like violence has a clear threshold, a line you can point to and say, "There. That's too far."

But it doesn't work that way when you're inside it.

When you grow up around harm, your threshold for "too far" isn't where it should be. You normalise, you excuse, you minimise. You say things like:

"Well, he didn't hit me this time, he just yelled."

"Well, he didn't punch me, he just shoved me."

"Well, he said sorry after."

"Well, I've had worse."

You shift the line so many times that by the time you're being strangled or kicked after surgery, a part of you is still saying, I can handle this. I've handled worse.

That's the horror of it.

The caravan wasn't physically the worst thing he ever did to me.

But psychologically, it was the moment the story I had been telling myself finally stopped working.

I couldn't convince myself he was "just angry."

I couldn't pretend he "lost control."

I couldn't hold the fantasy of being special to him.

Because if you're special to someone, they don't headbutt you in a caravan in front of strangers, threaten your safety, then leave you to fend for yourself in the dark.

You don't have to be a psychologist to see it.

You just have to finally stop lying to yourself.

That night, the lie died.

The relationship didn't end in that moment.

The fantasy did.

Once the fantasy dies, staying becomes harder than leaving.

***

Survival Is Not Always Running — Sometimes It's Strategy

From the outside, people think survival looks like:

grabbing your bags

calling the police

marching out the door in one dramatic exit.

Sometimes it does.

But more often, survival looks like what I did the morning after the caravan:

Get up when he says get up.

Don't argue.

Don't provoke.

Don't try to process emotions with someone who has none for you.

Keep your voice even.

Keep your face neutral.

Do what you need to do to get to your vehicle, your house, your life.

I wasn't "weak" because I got in his car that morning.

I was strategic.

I knew I needed him calm enough to drive me to my truck.

I knew he could turn on me again in a heartbeat.

I knew that if I pushed, if I fought back, if I demanded accountability, he could switch from sullen to explosive in seconds.

Strong women don't always fight in obvious ways.

Sometimes strength is in the women who play along until they are safe enough to walk away.

Sometimes strength is silent.

That morning, I did exactly what I needed to do to survive:

I didn't wake the monster.

I helped with a few tasks.

I stayed neutral.

I kept my eyes on the goal: keys, truck, home, gone.

On paper, it might look like compliance.

In reality, it was an exit strategy.

***

Why I Didn't Tell Anyone

This is the part people struggle to understand:

"Why didn't you tell someone?"

"Why didn't you ask for help?"

Because shame.

Because denial.

Because I was still trying to reconcile the two versions of myself:

the strong, don't-mess-with-me woman I'd always been, and

the woman who had spent years going back to a man who treated her like shit.

How do you explain that?

How do you say:

"I'm smart, I'm capable, I've survived so much already... and yet this man can turn me inside out with one text message?"

How do you admit:

"I stayed. Not once. Not twice. Over and over again."

You don't.

You put on your mask.

You make jokes.

You say, "Yeah, it was bad, but I'm fine now."

You tell half-truths because the full truth makes *you* cringe.

I didn't stay silent to protect him.

I stayed silent because I couldn't stand the reflection of myself I thought I'd see in other people's eyes.

Weak.

Stupid.

Pathetic.

None of which were true.

But that's what shame does — it turns a trauma response into a character flaw.

This silence is one of the most universal patterns in DV — not because women want to hide the truth, but because they don't want to face what the truth says about their reality.

***

The Quiet After the Storm

When I finally drove away from his house that morning, the breaking point had happened long before I turned the key in the ignition.

There was no dramatic moment, no cinematic collapse of everything I'd been holding together.

Just a quiet, razor-sharp clarity settling over me like cold air.

There were no raised voices.

No final battle to win or lose.

No performance to endure.

Just the stillness that comes when the soul has already decided it's done.

I didn't leave because of a single incident.

I left because something deep inside me stopped arguing with the truth.

Stopped bargaining.

Stopped pretending I could hold together a relationship that had been rotting from the inside.

REFLECTION

The grief that followed wasn't for him.

It was for the lies I had wrapped myself in.

For the years I spent defending a version of us that never existed.

For the pieces of myself I kept sacrificing to keep hope alive.

People imagine the breaking point as a violent snap — but sometimes it's nothing more than an exhale.

A surrender.

A moment where you finally admit that love cannot survive on promises and potential.

The real ending didn't happen on the road.

It happened inside me, in the shift from denial to knowing.

In the quiet, devastating acceptance that the relationship I kept trying to rescue was already gone.

And once you see that truth, you can't unsee it.

You can only walk away.

***

What I Want Other Women to Know

If you are still in it, or just out of it, and you're judging yourself for not leaving "earlier," I want you to hear this clearly:

You stayed because:

your nervous system was wired from childhood to endure

you were trauma-bonded to someone who knew exactly how to hook you back in

you were trained to see harm as normal and kindness as suspicious

you believed, deep down, that if you loved him enough, he would change.

You stayed because you're loyal.

Because you're hopeful.

Because you're compassionate.

Because you wanted the story to have a different ending.

Those qualities aren't flaws.

They're beautiful parts of you that someone weaponised.

The breaking point isn't a single perfect moment of bravery.

It's a thousand small realisations piling up until one day, your body, your heart, your soul all agree:

No fucking more.

The caravan was my moment.

Yours might look different.

It might be the first time he scares your child.

The first time he threatens to hurt your pet.

The first time you see hatred in his eyes instead of anger.

The first time you realise you've become someone you don't recognise.

Whatever it is, it counts.

You don't need a broken bone or a newspaper headline to justify leaving.

You only need that bone-deep knowing:

"If I stay, I will lose myself."

"If I keep doing this, I may lose my life."

That knowing is your turning point.

Even if it takes you a while to act on it.

Even if you wobble.

Even if you go back once, twice, ten times.

When that truth arrives and settles in your soul, something in you is already walking toward the exit.

The rest of the story — the collapse, the healing, the rebuilding, the woman you become — is born from that moment.

And that is why the breaking point matters. Not because it was the worst thing that happened to you, but because it was the moment you finally believed you deserved to live.

IV

THE AFTERMATH & HEALING

Chapter 1

*"Sometimes the first step out of hell is simply lying
down long enough to recognise you're still alive."*

How breaking apart became the first step toward reclaiming myself.

The morning I drove home, something in me felt resolved in a way I hadn't felt in years.

I walked into my house — my sanctuary — and was hit by a wave of gratitude so fierce it almost buckled me. Gratitude that I had never moved in with him. Gratitude that I had a door he couldn't walk through without permission. Gratitude that I had made it home at all.

Then the exhaustion hit.

Not tiredness.

A bone-deep collapse.

I curled up on my bed, turned on a TV show, and stayed there.

Not for a day.

Not for a week.

For months.

***

The Two-World Split

On the outside, I functioned.

51

I went to work.

I paid bills.

I did the basic chores that kept life running.

But the second the essentials were done, I retreated straight back to bed like a creature hiding in a cave. My bed became my refuge and my prison — the place I escaped to and the place I slowly unravelled in.

Food became both comfort and punishment, a way to soothe the ache and fill the space he'd carved out of me. Showering turned into something I did only when I started to smell myself or when my hair became an oil slick. My standards slipped because my spirit had slipped. In that moment, I didn't have the energy to pull any of it back together.

I wasn't in physical pain anymore — the bruises faded, the swelling went down — but emotionally, I was living inside a storm that never stopped.

***

The Mental Torture

For five months, my mind became a battlefield.

I oscillated wildly between longing and hatred — between wanting him to knock on my door whispering that he'd changed… and wanting him to catch some horrific STD that made his pecker fall off.

I'm not proud of the thought, but trauma does that — it drags you to dark, contradictory places where you can pray for someone and curse them at the same time.

I looked for him everywhere — scanning highways, passing cars, carparks — terrified I'd see him, yet craving it.

I talked to him constantly in my head.

Long speeches.

Angry rants.

Imagined reunions.

Fantasies of him apologising.

Fantasies of me finally telling him he was the biggest prick on earth.

CHAPTER 1

Sleep barely came.
My mind wouldn't shut up.
Five months of intrusive thoughts, looping memories, and mental torture.
I replayed every woman I'd caught him cheating with.
Every lie.
Every assault.
Every moment I should have walked away.
It wasn't healing.
It was survival — forcing myself to stay angry so I wouldn't go back.

***

The Embodied Aftermath
My body didn't let me forget.
The goose egg on my forehead lingered under my fringe. The bruises covered by winter clothes. The headaches — which I'd never had before him — became a regular part of my life. Nightmares followed me into the early hours. I slept in patches, if at all.
My adrenal system gave out completely.
I started passing out from stress.
Having panic attacks while driving.
Sitting in the doctor's office convinced my congenital heart condition had worsened.
Turned out it wasn't my heart.
It was adrenal exhaustion — years of living on high alert, years of shrinking during explosions, years of sleeping beside danger.
My body had been bracing for so long it no longer knew how to exist without tension.

***

The Shame and the Silence
I told almost no one what was happening inside me. Two friends knew pieces — but never the full picture. I made jokes about the rest.

Downplayed. Minimised. Hid.
Not to protect him.
To protect myself.
From judgement.
From the question every abused woman dreads:
"Why didn't you just leave?"
They didn't know that leaving a violent man isn't a decision — it's a strategy. A risk. A calculation of what might get you killed.
They didn't know the trauma bond was still gripping me tight.
And beneath it all sat shame.
A thick, choking shame.
Because I wasn't the kind of woman who tolerated this shit.
Or so I'd always believed.
I'd been strong my whole life.
Tough.
Direct.
Don't-mess-with-me energy.
And yet with this man, every boundary, every conviction, every ounce of self-preservation had been eroded piece by piece. That contradiction carved me open. It made me feel weak, stupid, disposable.
There were nights I didn't want to be alive anymore.
Not because I wanted to die —
but because I couldn't keep living in the fallout.

***

December — The Return

Early December, he turned up at my house.
Just walked in like a ghost out of the past.
He was nervous — I could see it.
And that softness hit me right in the chest.
Trauma bonds do that. They make you mistake familiarity for destiny.
The cynical part of me thought, *Right. Someone's dumped him. Here we*

CHAPTER 1

go again.
    The wounded part of me still wanted to believe he chose me.
    We talked for a couple of days after his visit. It felt familiar.
    Addictive.
    Like slipping back into an old drug.
    And then — two days in — he went cold.
    I recognised it immediately.
    His tells.
    The change in tone.
    The divided attention.
    He'd lined up someone else.
    I knew it as surely as I knew my own name.
    Something in me recoiled.
    My stomach dropped.
    My body said *no* before my brain caught up.
    I told him I couldn't do it.
    That nothing had changed.
    That I was done.
    He blew up on the phone — but not having him physically near me made all the difference.
    I hung up, feeling sick and exhausted.
    This time, I didn't go back.

Chapter 2

*"When no hand reaches back, you
learn the strength of your own."*

The System That Wasn't There

Leaving is supposed to be the end of the story.

People imagine that once you walk out the door, the worst is behind you — that safety arrives instantly, that help appears, that everything broken inside you miraculously heals.

But leaving is not the end.

It is the beginning of a different kind of survival, a different kind of hell.

In the days after I finally left, my body was free, but the rest of me was still trapped in the aftermath — the fear, the looping thoughts, the silence.

You don't walk out of a DV relationship with a clean slate. You walk out with invisible wounds that no one sees and a nervous system that still braces for impact long after the danger is gone.

The Police DV unit looking after my case connected me to the correct support systems, the officer assigned to my case was incredibly helpful — the intake services, the safety networks, the therapy waitlists, the organisations designed to help women like me, had no availability for months.

CHAPTER 2

Not days.
Not weeks.
Months.
Nine months passed before the phone finally rang.
By then, I had rebuilt myself alone.
I wasn't angry at the woman on the other end of the line. She sounded tired in a way only someone on the frontlines of domestic violence can sound — worn down by the weight of trying to save too many women with too little time, too little funding, too little support. Her voice carried a kind of weary compassion that comes from hearing the same stories on repeat, day after day.
The problem wasn't her.
It wasn't the police who did their job with care.
It was the sheer volume of women needing help — all of us trying to climb out of the same fire.
Most people don't know this part of the story.
They assume help is immediate.
That when a woman leaves, a net is waiting to catch her.
But the truth is brutal: the system is overwhelmed.
So many women are reaching out that the net is frayed and thinning, and far too often, it does not catch us in time.
I declined the appointment when it finally arrived, not out of pride, but because I was already stitching myself together. I had learned to quiet my own panic and rebuild my own life.
But I have never forgotten what those long wait months meant — how easily the ending of this story could have been different. How many women do not survive long enough to receive that call.
This is where my real healing began: not in a clinic or a counselling room, but in the moments I learned to mother myself, to steady myself, to rise without being rescued. I did not heal because help arrived.
I healed because I refused to disappear.

And this part of the story — the rebuilding, the reclaiming, the slow and stubborn becoming — is just as important as the escape.

Because leaving is survival.

Healing is resurrection.

Chapter 3

"The day you choose yourself is the day your life begins again."

The Resurrection

The day everything changed didn't look dramatic from the outside.
It was January 12th. Five months after the collapse.
A date that will sit in my memory the way some people hold anniversaries — not of love, but of return.
I woke up with a clarity that felt almost foreign, like someone had reached into my chest overnight and flipped a switch labelled enough.
No heaviness dragging at my limbs.
Just a calm, grounded certainty.
This isn't going to be my life.
Not another year.
Not another month.
Not another day.
And then I got out of bed and moved like a woman possessed.
There was no easing into it.
No gentle transition.
No "start small" self-help bullshit.
I went full tilt, the way I tackle everything when I finally decide.
I changed everything in a single day.
I cleaned out the cupboards and my fridge.

I threw away the junk.

I made a juice, then a smoothie, then prepped vegetables like I was feeding a small army.

I went full vegan for the first few weeks — fruit, vegetables, beans, lentils — not because of some moral obligation, but because I wanted to cleanse every part of him out of my body.

I wanted my cells back.

I went out into my garden — the place I had abandoned during the worst of it — and planted two full beds of fresh greens. A literal future I could watch grow. Something alive that depended on me, not the other way around.

And that same morning, with the smell of soil still on my hands, I sat down and opened a blank document, and I started writing.

The dream I had buried, the dream of being a published author.

The story poured out of me like it had been waiting for the door to open.

I mothered myself that day.

Showered.

Dressed properly.

Brushed my hair.

Spoke kindly to myself — not in some performative way, but in a quiet, grounded, "I'm not abandoning you" way.

My house was always clean — that had never slipped — but that day, it felt like a place to rebuild. A place with walls no one else could step through uninvited.

And then came the nature.

Hiking three times a week with a client I'd just started training.

Push-bike riding.

Swimming.

Kayaking.

Movement became medicine.

CHAPTER 3

Sunlight became oxygen.

Sweat became therapy.

It was the first time in years that my body wasn't bracing for impact. It was moving for me.

But healing isn't linear. Not ever.

People love the clean narrative — the triumphant turning point, the fresh start, the happily-ever-after of self-resurrection.

That's not how it went.

Even after January 12th, I thought about him almost every day.

Not with longing — the crying had stopped; the nightmares were gone — but with a looping curiosity I couldn't fully shake.

Where is he?

Who is he with?

Does he think of me?

Did I matter at all?

Would he show up on my doorstep again?

I didn't want him back.

But my nervous system didn't know that yet.

Trauma bonds don't dissolve on command.

They loosen slowly, like a rope that's been pulled too tight and begins to fray strand by strand.

My mind still played tricks on me — daydreams, mental conversations, intrusive flashes of memory.

Sometimes I'd swear I saw his truck on the highway and my stomach would drop.

Hope and disgust lived side by side inside me.

Longing and revulsion.

Relief and grief.

I wasn't emotionally broken anymore, but I wasn't free either.

Not yet.

And still — I didn't waver.

I didn't relapse.
I didn't contact him.
I didn't spiral back into the cycle.
I didn't look him up or reach out.
I stayed busy.
Brutally busy.
Obsessively busy.
Diet.
Exercise.
Nature.
Writing.
Building my author business.
Creating.
Working.
Reclaiming every piece of myself he had eroded.
I lost the weight.
My strength returned.
My body came back into itself.
My routines stabilised.
My spirit lifted.
But recovery isn't only measured in the return of the body.
It's measured in the quiet moments — the ones where the mind tries to drag you back and you don't follow.
Those first months were not joyful.
They were disciplined.
Focused.
Determined.
I fought myself harder than I ever fought him.
And I was winning.
Until May.
When he showed up at my house again.

CHAPTER 3

But that is the next chapter.
Because rebuilding doesn't happen without being tested.

Chapter 4

*"The test of healing isn't whether the past returns —
it's whether it still has a hold on you."*

The Test: When the Past Knocks Again

Healing will always test you.

Not with a gentle nudge, but with the exact thing that once broke you — showing up uninvited, standing on your doorstep, daring you to slip back into the old story.

For me, that test came in May.

It was an ordinary afternoon.

I was writing — fully immersed in the world of *Witchborn* — the first thing in years that had given me purpose, momentum, direction. I was deep in the scene, the kind of focus where the rest of the world falls away.

My door was open as it always is, and I heard "Hey".

I knew that voice. My entire body went rigid.

I looked up and saw him standing there, it felt like time folded in on itself.

Not in the romantic movie sense.

In the what the actual fuck sense.

He talked for five minutes — about his work, his life, nothing personal — and it was obvious he wasn't here for me. He didn't ask how I'd been.

CHAPTER 4

He didn't ask about my life, my healing, my world.
  It hit me in a way it never had before:
  He had never been curious about me.
  Not once.
  Not ever.
  It had always been him at the centre.
  His life.
  His needs.
  His feelings.
  His drama.
  I had never been equal.
And somehow, I'd never seen it clearly until he was standing on my doorstep like an echo from a life I'd already outgrown.
  When he asked for a hug, I hesitated for half a second — not out of fear, but out of instinct. But I agreed, because I didn't want any hassles, and because part of me wanted to see what my body would do.
  The moment my arms wrapped around him, something clicked — silently, unmistakably.
  He felt like a stranger.
  Not familiar.
  Not comforting.
  Not warm.
  Just... foreign.
  It didn't feel like coming home.
  It didn't feel like love.
  It didn't even feel like history.
  It felt like hugging a man I had once known who now meant nothing to me.
  No spark.
  No ache.
  No longing.

Nothing.

And in that moment — more than any breakdown, any bruise, any sleepless night, any boundary I'd crawled across — I realised something powerful:

The trauma bond had finally cracked.

Because the body never lies.

My mind still thought about him sometimes, still looped old thoughts, still replayed old nightmares that weren't nightmares anymore — but my body?

My body was done.

The pull was gone.

The chemical hook was gone.

The illusion was gone.

He stepped back, said he had to go.

No conversation about what he'd done.

No accountability.

Just a parting line about how he'd been thinking of me.

And then he walked away.

I watched him leave, my heart strangely quiet.

That was the moment I knew I was healing.

Not because I didn't feel sadness or anger or grief anymore.

Not because I had forgiven him.

Not because everything was perfect.

But because the cord had snapped.

Something in me had shifted.

The spell was broken.

The man who once controlled my fear, my heart, my thoughts, my body —

was now nothing more than a man I used to know.

The danger was still real.

The memories still existed.

CHAPTER 4

The trauma was still unwinding itself inside me.
But the hold?
Gone.
Healing doesn't announce itself with fireworks.
Sometimes it arrives quietly —
in the moment you hug the person who once destroyed you,
and your body whispers:
No more.
That five-minute visit didn't set me back.
It confirmed my direction.
I wasn't his anymore.
I wasn't who I was with him.
I wasn't even who I had been after I'd left.
I was becoming someone new.
Someone stronger.
Someone whole.
Someone who could look danger in the face and feel nothing but clarity.
And that — more than anything — was the first moment I truly believed I was going to be okay.

Chapter 5

"A woman becomes unstoppable the moment she learns the difference between protecting herself and rediscovering herself."

Rebuilding the Woman Beneath the Warrior

Healing didn't make me softer.
If anything, it clarified me.
People think survivors become fragile in the aftermath — shaky, timid, afraid.
But I've never been that woman. Not before him. Not during him. Not after.
I don't flinch.
I never have.
Not even when I should have.
When danger comes at me, I rise.
When someone tries to control me, I push back.
Even in the relationship, I stood my ground. I yelled back. I hit back. I refused to cower. My reactions didn't stop the violence — sometimes they escalated it — but they were never born of weakness. They were born of a lifetime of surviving by resisting.
So, the months after leaving weren't about learning to be brave.
I'd been brave my whole life.
They were about learning to be wise.

CHAPTER 5

To see the difference between:
fighting to survive
and
fighting for myself.
Between:
standing up to him
and
standing up for me.
Between:
being reactive
and
being rooted.

This was the first time in my life I wasn't in a constant defensive stance.

I finally had space — real internal space — to study myself without trying to outrun someone else's temper.

And what I discovered was confronting.

I realised I'd never actually had the luxury of understanding myself before.

Not in childhood.

Not in adulthood.

Not in the relationship.

Everything had always been about surviving the next event, the next emotion, the next explosion.

Now there was silence.

And that silence forced honesty.

I began tracing back my patterns — the way I tolerated things that should have been non-negotiable, the way I mistook intensity for connection, the way I kept trying to fix broken people like it was my purpose.

It wasn't self-blame.

It was self-study — the first real study I'd ever done of myself.

For once, I wasn't analysing him.

I was analysing me.

And that's where the compassion began.

I had spent years being hard on myself — calling myself stupid for staying, weak for forgiving, naïve for hoping. But when I started looking at my history with clear eyes, the truth landed differently:

I didn't stay because I was weak.

I stayed because strength was the only tool I'd ever had.

Strength to survive.

Strength to fight back.

Strength to rationalise.

Strength to endure what should have broken me.

I fought because no one else ever fought for me.

I stood my ground because I was conditioned to stand alone.

I tried to fix him because I'd spent my whole life cleaning up other people's damage.

Understanding that didn't excuse anything I'd done.

But it explained everything I'd felt.

And that explanation opened the door to something I had never truly given myself:

Grace.

Not the soft, fluffy kind.

The grounded kind.

The kind that says:

"You did what you knew how to do. And now you're learning something different."

As the months unfolded, connection became another part of the rebuild — not the frantic connection of trauma, but deliberate, chosen connection.

I reopened relationships I had withdrawn from.

CHAPTER 5

I let friends back in.

I repaired strained bonds in small, honest ways.

I allowed myself to be supported — something I hadn't done in decades.

I realised how many people had been waiting for me to return.

Not the version of me he had shaped.

Not the exhausted, diminished, hollowed-out woman I had become.

Me.

The me who laughs loudly.

The me who speaks plainly.

The me who doesn't apologise for taking up space.

The me who stands firm without needing to fight.

Rebuilding wasn't a grand renaissance.

It wasn't a movie montage.

It wasn't a spiritual awakening.

It was a slow excavation — brushing dust off the parts of myself I had forgotten, uncovering instincts that had gone dormant, and learning what worth actually felt like when it wasn't based on survival.

The woman emerging wasn't new.

She wasn't reinvented.

She wasn't "healed" in the way people romanticise.

She was revealed.

The woman beneath the warrior —

the one who had existed long before him,

the one he never managed to break,

the one who was waiting for me to stop surviving long enough to finally meet her.

Chapter 6

*"Hindsight is the lantern that lights the path
we kept stumbling through in the dark."*

Looking Back: The Red Flags Were Loud
I didn't understand the pattern back then. I only felt the consequences.
But trauma makes you look backward differently — with clearer eyes, clearer memory, clearer truth.
And when I do that now, I can see the signs I missed.
The red flags that were loud long before the violence ever was.

***

The Way He Looked at Other Women
Not a quick glance.
Not a normal "oh she's pretty."
He clocked women.
Head to toe.
Slow.
Measuring.
Taking them in like he was inventorying them.
And when she walked past again?
He'd do it again.
I'd be mid-sentence and watch his eyes slide off me and latch onto

someone else across the room. The way his head physically turned to follow them told me more about his priorities than anything he ever said.

It wasn't just disrespect.

It felt like I was the interim until something better came along.

***

The Entertainment He Considered 'Normal'

Early in the relationship, he got me to watch movies he called "classics."

Both were about women being kept naked in cages, humiliated, abused, broken.

He watched them laughing and pointing, like it was normal entertainment.

I remember telling him they were traumatising — that I didn't understand why he thought they were "great."

Looking back now, that detail alone was a red flag waving like a motherfucker.

***

The Shallow Conversation That Never Went Anywhere

He could talk for hours —

but only if the conversation centred on him.

On the surface, he did ask about my day, my hopes, my dreams.

He'd nod, offer a half-hearted "that's good," pretend to be supportive.

But the disinterest was always there.

I'd be mid-sentence and he'd:

talk over me

suddenly start a story about himself

interrupt with something trivial

lose focus and stare at the TV

or drift so far internally I may as well have been speaking to a wall.

It was politeness masquerading as connection.

His work.
His mates.
His motorbikes.
His wants.
His irritations.
His weekend plans.

I didn't realise at first that his curiosity about me was surface-level only — just enough to appear like a boyfriend, but never enough to actually be present.

I'm naturally warm and curious — I give people space, I listen deeply, I care.

But looking back, it was always unbalanced.
No building anything together.
No emotional depth or true intimacy.
Just empty space where connection should have been.
It wasn't that he never asked —
it's that he never *listened*.

***

Being Told I Was "Too Sensitive"

Every time something hurt, or didn't feel right, or crossed a boundary, he had the same line:
"You're too sensitive."
Translation:
Your feelings make my life inconvenient.
It wasn't just minimising — it was conditioning.
Teaching me to doubt my own perceptions.
Teaching me to swallow anything that didn't flatter him.
I learned quickly that if I had a need, it would be dismissed.
So, I stopped having needs.

***

His Words Never Matched His Actions

CHAPTER 6

He always said the right things.
But his behaviour?
A completely different story.
He'd promise time together, then vanish.
Say he loved and adored me, then go and cheat.
Say he wanted a future, then make zero effort to build one.
Say I mattered — right before smacking me in the head.
I kept believing the words.
But it was his actions telling the truth.

***

The Intimacy That Never Existed
This was a red flag I didn't recognise for a long time.
He didn't want intimacy — not physical, not emotional, not sensual.
Most of the time, it didn't work at all.
And when I tried to discuss it gently — no blame, no pressure — he shut down.
I'd say:
"We can try different things. What do you enjoy? What feels good for you?"
He'd say:
"It's not you, it's my body."
But the truth was impossible to ignore:
His body worked perfectly fine for cheating.
It wasn't just the lack of sex —
it was the way he pulled away from every form of closeness.
If I wore lingerie, he'd avert his eyes like I wasn't even standing there.
Sometimes he'd literally look around me to watch TV and tell me I was "in the way."
He slept fully clothed — head to toe — while I slept naked beside him.
The physical barrier said everything.
And he'd cuddle the dog instead of me.

I loved the hound, but it stung —
how he'd offer warmth to a dog but not to the woman lying next to him.
It felt telling.
It felt personal.
It felt like rejection wrapped in routine.
Lack of intimacy with me wasn't physical.
It was emotional withholding.
Avoidance.
Dismissal.
And yes — it was deeply, deeply demoralising.

***

I Wasn't Being Chosen
Not truly.
Not deeply.
Not emotionally.
He wanted company.
He wanted attention.
He wanted admiration.
He wanted control.
He wanted me available.
But he didn't want me.
Not the way I deserved to be wanted.
That was the real red flag — the one I only understand now.
I kept trying to make myself "good enough," "calm enough," "sexy enough," "understanding enough."
But no version of me would have been chosen.
Because it was never about my worth.
It was about his emptiness.

***

The Little Lies That Became Big Ones

CHAPTER 6

In the beginning, it was small lies — tiny inconsistencies that didn't make sense.

Details that didn't add up.

Statements said with such casual confidence that I doubted my own memory.

A white lie here.

A twisted detail there.

Nothing "big" enough to confront on its own.

I'd catch him out sometimes, and he'd shrug.

Laugh.

Or flip it back onto me like I was imagining things.

I didn't realise I was watching the warm-up act.

Because those little lies were practice.

Rehearsal.

Grooming.

The prelude to the whoppers so outrageous I'd question my own sanity trying to make sense of them.

Lies about where he was.

Lies about who he was with.

Lies about women.

Lies about prostitutes.

Lies about money.

Lies about everything.

Looking back now, the white lies were the opening note.

The overture.

The beginning of the end.

These were the warnings.

Seeing them for what they were freed me in ways leaving him never could.

Chapter 7

*"Where fear and love are taught in the same breath,
the heart mistakes survival for devotion."*

The Psychology of Survival

People talk about domestic violence like it's a series of bad decisions,
or a lack of boundaries,
or a weakness in women who "should have known better."
They don't understand the psychology of it —
the way it rewires you,
the way it hooks you,
the way it uses every scar from your past as an anchor point.
I didn't understand it either.
Not until I was out.
Not until I had distance.
Not until the fog began to lift and I started seeing my patterns.
This chapter isn't about him.
It's about the machinery behind the cycle —
the psychology that keeps women stuck and silent
long after the bruises fade.
It's the part experts rarely explain well
and the part survivors rarely have the language for
until they claw their way through the fire and look back at the

wreckage
with clear eyes.
This is what I learned.

***

The Nervous System Doesn't Know "Love." It Knows "Familiar."
People assume we stay because of romance.
That's bullshit.
The nervous system does not bond to "love."
It bonds to patterns.
When you grow up in upheaval —
yelling, threats, fear, conditional affection —
your body learns a simple, primal rule:
Unsafe feels normal.
Stable feels suspicious.
Calm feels foreign.
So, when a man arrives wrapped in intensity —
big emotions, big declarations, big reactions —
your body says:
Ah. I know this.
I've danced this rhythm before.
Your mind calls it connection.
Your body calls it survival.
That's not weakness.
That's conditioning.

***

The Trauma Bond Is Not Emotional, It's Chemical
This is the truth no one explains properly:
A trauma bond is addiction.
Pure biology.
The cycle of:
affection

tension
explosion
apology
creates a chemical loop in your brain.
Dopamine → Cortisol → Adrenaline → Oxytocin
Over and over.
It's the same pattern that forms between prisoners and captors.
It's the same pattern that forms in childhood when love and fear come from the same person.
Your body becomes dependent on:
the high of the apology
the relief after the fear
the tiny crumbs of affection
the unpredictable cycle that keeps you chasing stability you will never receive

So, when people ask:
"Why didn't you just leave?"
It's like asking a drug addict why they didn't "just stop."
The chemistry is stronger than the logic.
And the abuser knows that.
Intuitively.
Instinctively.
Sometimes consciously.
They feed you just enough to keep the hook in.
They take just enough to dismantle you.

***

The Grooming: How Abusers Train You Without You Realising
Abusers don't start with violence.
They start with:
intensity
attention

CHAPTER 7

vulnerability
connection
fantasy-building
He mirrors your values.
Matches your pace.
Reflects your dreams back to you.
He makes you feel chosen.
That's not an accident.
That's grooming.
Then the cracks come.
Tiny ones.
Insignificant on their own.
A cancelled plan.
A small lie.
A subtle withdrawal.
A shift in tone that makes you question what you did wrong.
And because you're empathetic —
because you've spent your life managing other people's emotional weather —
you try to fix it.
Every violent man relies on the same formula:
Break her confidence.
Feed her hope.
Repeat.
By the time the violence appears,
you're already conditioned to question yourself
instead of him.

***

The Internal Split: When Two Truths Collide
Here's the part only survivors understand:
You don't stay with the man who hurts you.

You stay with the man he pretended to be.
The brain holds both versions at once:
the charming man
the violent man
And your nervous system swings between them, desperate to reconcile the two.
You tell yourself:
"He didn't mean it."
"He can change."
"He was abused too."
"He's good underneath."
"He loves me."
"I can fix this."
"I made him angry."
These aren't excuses.
These are survival strategies.
Your brain is trying to make sense of danger while clinging to the illusion of safety.
The contradiction itself becomes the prison.

***

The Four Lies Every Survivor Tells Herself
I didn't learn these from books.
I learned them from bleeding, crying, surviving, refusing to die.
Lie 1: "It's not that bad."
Minimisation is armour.
If you acknowledge the truth,
you have to act on it —
and that action might get you killed.
Lie 2: "He can change."
This one is compassion weaponised.
Your empathy becomes the chain around your own neck.

Lie 3: "I can handle it."
This is the lie strong women tell.
And it's the one that keeps them alive long enough to escape.
Lie 4: "He won't kill me."
This is the most dangerous lie of all.
It's the lie I told myself
while looking at the man who later admitted he'd dump my body in a lake.
You don't see death clearly
when hope is still standing in front of it.

***

Why Leaving Is Not a Decision — It's a Strategy
The world believes leaving is a choice.
It isn't.
It is:
timing
calculation
risk management
emotional preparation
physical opportunity
financial safety
geographic safety
psychological detachment
Women don't leave when they're fed up.
They leave when:
the hope dies
the denial breaks
the body finally rebels
the danger becomes undeniable
they see their own death clearly
the bond loosens just enough to make space for clarity.

Leaving is not a moment.
It is a process.
Mine began the night in the caravan.
It ended the morning I drove away.
But the real work — the disentangling — came after.

**

The Final Truth: You Survive Because You Are Strong, Not Weak
(read that again, slowly)
People think strong women never end up in violent relationships.
They're wrong.
Strong women survive them.
We fight back.
We stand our ground.
We try to fix the unfixable.
We endure the unimaginable.
We love with depth.
We hope with ferocity.
We survive where others would crumble.
Strength doesn't protect you from violence.
Strength helps you walk out alive.
And the psychology of survival isn't about weakness —
it's about adaptation.
Women like me don't stay because we're fragile.
We stay because we've been conditioned to endure
and trained from childhood to navigate danger
with courage, intelligence, instinct, and fire.
The healing happens when you learn to use that fire for yourself
instead of burning yourself alive to keep someone else warm.
This chapter — this understanding —
was the turning point where my story stopped being about him
and started being about me.

CHAPTER 7

Because survival is instinct.
But healing?
Healing is a choice.
And I chose myself.

Chapter 8

*"What breaks you is not what defines you;
what you reclaim is."*

Reclaiming Identity & Worth

There comes a moment in healing where survival isn't the goal anymore.

Where getting out of bed, eating properly, and not collapsing under memories is no longer the victory.

Where the question shifts from:

"How do I stay alive?"

to

"Who am I now?"

This chapter is about that moment.

The reclamation.

The remembering.

The reconstruction of a self I had abandoned long before the violence ever began.

Because the truth is this:

I didn't lose myself in that relationship.

I lost myself long before it —

and leaving him simply forced me to confront it.

That was the real work.

CHAPTER 8

The work no one prepares you for.
The work that strips you down to bone and then asks you who you want to be
when no one is defining you through fear.

***

The Identity Beneath The Armour
For most of my life, I believed my strength was my identity.
I was the fighter.
The one who stood my ground.
The one who didn't flinch.
The one who wasn't afraid of anyone.
It was a truth —
but it wasn't the whole truth.
Because strength built from survival
is not the same as strength built from self-worth.
One is reactive.
One is foundational.
Leaving him forced me to see the difference.
For the first time in decades, I wasn't fighting anyone.
Not a partner.
Not a parent.
Not the ghosts of my childhood.
And without someone else's crap to push against,
my identity began to crack open in ways I never expected.
I realised survival had shaped me —
but it had also limited me.
I had been strong
because I had never been allowed to be soft.
I had been fierce
because gentleness had been dangerous.
I had been guarded

because vulnerability had always been exploited.
For the first time, I began to wonder:
Who am I when I am not defending myself?
Who am I when I am not reacting?
Who am I when I am finally free?
The answers didn't come quickly.
They arrived slowly, in layers —
a reclaiming of self-permission I'd never had before.

***

The Rediscovery of Want
Survival had trained me to think in terms of needs:
safety
food
calm
protection
escape
stability
But once the dust settled, another question emerged —
one I hadn't asked since I was a teenager:
What do I want?
Not what do I tolerate.
Not what do I endure.
Not what do I settle for.
What do I actually *fucking* want?
And answering that was harder than leaving him.
Because wanting requires self-worth.
Wanting requires believing you deserve something more than the bare minimum.
Wanting requires admitting how long you have lived without it.
Slowly, I began remembering parts of myself I'd abandoned:
the woman who loves adventure

the woman who thrives in nature
the woman who creates worlds on a page
the woman who feels deeply
the woman who dreams big
the woman who values loyalty, intellect, humour
the woman who will not shrink for anyone
the woman who will move mountains for those she loves.
These weren't "new" pieces.
They were the original pieces —
the ones buried under conditioning and pain.
Reclaiming them felt like returning to myself after a long absence.

***

The Difference Between Being Strong and Being Whole
Strength kept me alive.
Wholeness let me move forward.
Strength says:
"I can survive anything."
Wholeness says:
"I no longer accept anything that threatens me."
Strength says:
"I don't need anyone."
Wholeness says:
"I deserve people who show up."
Strength says:
"I can handle it."
Wholeness says:
"I don't have to."
Wholeness was not something I had ever been taught.
It wasn't modelled for me growing up.
It wasn't something I believed I had the right to claim.
But healing forced me to recognise a truth I had never spoken aloud:

Being unbreakable doesn't make you safe.
Being whole does.
And for the first time in my life, I wanted wholeness more than anything else.

***

The Return to Connection
During the relationship, he consumed everything —
my attention, my emotional bandwidth, my decision-making, my space.
When that ended, I expected loneliness.
Instead, I found a quiet invitation waiting for me —
the people in my life who had never stopped caring.
Rebuilding connection wasn't about recounting trauma.
It wasn't about getting sympathy.
It was about letting myself be seen again —
authentically, without the mask, without the shame.
I started:
spending more time with the people I love
reaching out to friends I'd withdrawn from
sharing small truths instead of excuses
laughing without fear of consequences
rebuilding trust slowly, deliberately
letting myself enjoy company without bracing for the cost.
For the first time in years, I felt like part of the world again.
Not a shadow lurking in the periphery of someone else's storm.
Connection reminded me of something trauma had stolen:
Belonging is supposed to feel safe.
Not expensive.

***

Boundaries: The Language of Self-Worth
Leaving taught me something vital:

CHAPTER 8

Boundaries aren't walls.
They're self-respect in action.
For years, my boundaries were reactive —
appearing only after someone hurt me.
But in rebuilding, boundaries became proactive:
No to toxic people.
No to emotional vampires.
No to anyone who demanded without giving.
No to chaos disguised as passion.
No to interruptions of my peace.
No to disrespect.
And the most important one:
No to anyone who made me doubt the truth I had earned with blood.
I no longer explain myself.
I no longer negotiate my needs.
I no longer apologise for protecting my life.
Boundaries became my fluency in self-worth —
something I had never been allowed to learn until now.

***

The Woman Who Emerged

By the time I reached this stage of rebuilding, something fundamental had shifted:
I was no longer surviving.
I was expanding.
I was no longer fighting.
I was choosing.
I was no longer recovering.
I was becoming.
The woman who walked out of that relationship was bruised, exhausted, and held together by willpower.
The woman who stands here now is:

self-defined
self-led
self-respecting
self-aware
self-trusting
self-rooted
She does not flinch.
She does not apologise for taking up space.
She does not shrink to keep the peace.
She does not settle for crumbs.
She does not tolerate what hurts her.
She does not build her worth on survival anymore.
She builds it on truth.
Her truth.
And that is the deepest reclaiming of all.

Chapter 9

"Love is not the risk — abandoning yourself is."

Trusting Again, On My Terms
Healing didn't make me afraid of love.
It made me selective.
It taught me something I should have learned decades earlier: being alone isn't scary. Choosing the wrong man is.
For fifteen months, I didn't want a relationship.
Not because I was closed off —
but because for the first time in my life, I wasn't looking for anyone to fill a space inside me.
I was full.
Steady.
Settled inside myself in a way I never had been.
And when you reach that point, the idea of letting someone into your life becomes a very different consideration.
Not "Will he choose me?"
but "Does he deserve access?"

***

What I Will Never Tolerate Again
My standards didn't just rise —
they evolved.

Violence?

Non-negotiable. One strike, and I'm gone.

But the red flags I see now are more subtle than that, woven into character, not crises:

hot-and-cold behaviour dressed up as mystery

instant intensity from someone who barely knows me

men who check out other women while I stand beside them

eyes that wander everywhere but my face during a conversation

negativity saturating every story they tell

shallow talk with no depth, no insight, no accountability

inconsistencies between words and actions

no interest in my wellbeing, no curiosity about me.

These are the quiet dealbreakers.

The ones that tell me everything I need to know long before anything dramatic happens.

I used to mistake intensity for chemistry.

Now?

I look for emotional maturity, because emotional immaturity is where violence begins.

***

What I Require Now

Peace.

Consistency.

A man who communicates like an adult, not a boy in a grown man's body.

Someone who knows how to have a disagreement without resorting to cruelty, withdrawal, or punishment.

Someone with emotional intelligence — not Instagram-meme intelligence — but genuine self-awareness.

Someone with depth.

Grounded.

CHAPTER 9

Honest.

Loyal.

Able to sit in their own discomfort without making it my responsibility.

I don't need perfection.

I need alignment.

***

Future Love: Not a Desperation, a Possibility

For over a year, I didn't want anyone.

Not a date.

Not a conversation.

Not a possibility.

Not intimacy.

It wasn't grief.

It wasn't fear.

It was freedom.

And then, quietly, something shifted.

Not a longing — just an openness. The soft thought:

One day, I could love again.

Not the way I loved before —

not through fantasy, hope, projection, or emotional starvation.

But in a way that is rooted in reality.

Online dating?

Absolutely not.

It feels like a digital swap meet for disposable connections — men who want sex, not substance; attention, not true intimacy.

If I meet someone, it will be through real life, real energy, real presence — not swipes and algorithms.

I'm open to love, but only a love that rises to meet me where I now stand.

***

Trust, Redefined
Trust used to be about believing someone else.
Now it's about believing myself.
Trusting:
my intuition
my body
my uneasiness
my observations
the shift in my stomach
the tightening in my chest
the voice inside me that says no.
Those signals saved my life long before I understood them.
I trust others — but I trust myself more.
I trust that I will never abandon myself again.
I trust that if something feels off, I'll listen the first time.
I trust that I can walk away early, easily, unapologetically.
Trust is no longer something I give away.
It's something a man earns slowly, over time, with consistency.

***

The Internal Shifts
Healing didn't make me guarded.
It made me discerning.
The shifts inside me are permanent:
I read energy instantly now.
I don't excuse behaviour that contradicts words.
I don't confuse intensity for connection.
I don't override my intuition.
I don't chase.
I don't justify.
I don't tolerate inconsistency.
I value calm over chemistry.

I value stability over sparks.
I value communication over performance.
I used to think boundaries were rules to keep others out.
Now I know boundaries are promises I make to myself.

***

The Final Truth of This Chapter
I am not waiting for anyone.
I am living.
And if someone enters that life one day,
he won't be the centre of it —
he'll be the man who fits beside a woman who rebuilt herself from the inside out.
Because I don't need a partner to feel like a whole woman anymore.
But if the right man comes along…
I will recognise him instantly —
not by how he makes my heart race,
but by how my nervous system stays calm in his presence.
That is what trust looks like now.
That is what love will look like for me next time.
And that is the future I am building toward —
not with hope,
but with certainty.

Reflection

"A story stops hurting when you learn why it was written."

There is a version of healing people like to imagine — soft, structured, supported by counsellors who hand you tools and frameworks and coping strategies.

My healing didn't look like that.

I didn't have a therapist.

I didn't have a program.

I had myself — and something unexpected that became one of the most powerful tools I ever held:

A journal my son had given me.

It was called *Mum — I Want to Know About Your Life.*

A simple gift.

A tender gesture.

He had no idea what he was handing me.

I didn't either.

But that journal became my therapy.

✵✵✵

The Journal With a Purpose — Not Just Truth, But Meaning

Before I ever wrote the first word, I made a decision:

If I was going to do this,

I wasn't just going to list memories.

REFLECTION

I wasn't just going to recount events.
I wasn't sugarcoating anything.
I was going to write with:
absolute honesty, and
the wisdom I'd gained from living through it.
Not just the what happened,
but the what it taught me.
Not just the pain,
but the patterns I finally understood.
Not just the trauma,
but the truth those experiences revealed.
For the first time in my life, I wasn't just remembering —
I was making sense of it.

***

Turning My Life into a Map — Instead of a Battlefield

Each page asked questions that dug straight into the spine of my history:
What shaped you?
Where did you learn strength?
What hurt you the most?
What did it teach you?
What do you want your children to understand about you?
And as I wrote, something profound happened:
Every chapter of my life came with a lesson I hadn't seen before.
The journal didn't just help me unpack the past —
it helped me interpret it.
I wasn't just writing as a mother.
I was writing as a woman who had survived everything she was now brave enough to articulate.
The healing wasn't in the storytelling.
It was in the understanding.

***

A Two-Month Conversation with Myself
For two months, I wrote every day.
Not to vent.
Not to complain.
But to translate my life into clarity.
I saw patterns I had been blind to.
I saw generational threads.
I saw where I'd learned to fight, where I'd learned to tolerate, where I'd learned to stay silent, where I'd learned to rise.
It was like watching my life unfold in a way that finally made sense — not chaotic, not fragmented, but whole.
My son thought he had given me a sentimental journal.
He gave me a mirror.
A mentor.
A roadmap.
He gave me the chance to meet myself fully —
not the wounded parts,
not the performing parts,
but the woman underneath everything.

***

The Lesson of Radical Self-Trust — Found in my Own Story
With each entry, I realised something I had never understood before:
My instincts had always been right.
My body had always known.
My reactions weren't crazy — they were trained responses to danger.
My boundaries weren't flawed — they had never been modelled for me.
My compassion wasn't weakness — it was survival turned inward.
Writing the truth and the lessons rebuilt my ability to trust myself.
Not blindly.

Not idealistically.
But accurately.
My story taught me that I am not fragile.
I am not foolish.
I am not broken.
I am perceptive.
I am resilient.
I am capable.
I am wise.
And every insight I gained from writing proved that I could trust the woman I was becoming.

**

Emotional Independence
The journal didn't just give me a place to release.
It gave me a place to reframe.
When I put my life on paper — honestly, fully, with meaning —
I stopped needing external validation.
Because once you understand the psychology behind your own story, other people's opinions stop mattering.
I wasn't looking for someone to agree with me.
I wasn't rewriting history to fit a narrative.
I wasn't asking for permission to heal.
I was documenting the truth
and the wisdom that came from surviving it.
That is emotional independence.

**

The Woman who Emerged
When I finished the journal, I realised something life-altering:
I had rewritten my identity.
Not by inventing someone new,
but by finally understanding the woman I already was.

I had stitched together:
the girl who endured,
the woman who fought,
the survivor who left,
and the human being who deserved love, safety, respect, and peace.
Violence didn't define me.
Leaving didn't define me.
Healing didn't define me.
Understanding did.
Understanding my past.
Understanding my patterns.
Understanding my worth.
Understanding my future.
Understanding myself.
The journal didn't just help me heal.
It helped me claim myself.
Completely.
Consciously.
Confidently.
This was the moment I finally realised
I had never been broken at all.
Just buried.
Distorted.
Interrupted.
And now — fully seen, fully known, fully understood —
I emerged whole.

V

THRIVING

Chapter 1

"The life you rebuild after ruin is often truer than the one you lost."

The Life That Returned to Me

Life on the other side of violence doesn't explode into colour all at once.

It softens.

It expands.

Today, my life feels nothing like the one I escaped.

It feels hopeful.

Peaceful.

Disciplined.

Calm.

Purpose-led.

Creative.

Joyful.

There are still days where a 'what if' drifts through my mind like a familiar draft under an old door. There are still moments where a delusion flickers back to life like a film reel someone forgot to turn off.

But now, I snap out of it quickly — not because I force myself to, but because my understanding is deeper.

My self-reflection sharper.

My compassion for myself wider.
And the world inside me a whole lot steadier.

***

The Book That Saved Me

Writing *Witchborn* didn't just keep me going —
it gave me something to move toward.

It gave me purpose to pour myself into when the intrusive thoughts were trying their hardest to drag me backwards.

It gave my mind a place to go that wasn't trauma, wasn't fear, wasn't looping memories.

It offered escape, yes — but more than that, it offered creation.

I stepped into a fictional world full of strong women and strong men —

characters built with integrity, morality, justice, loyalty.

People who walked in the light even when darkness clawed at their heels.

Without realising it at the start, I was writing the antidote to what I had lived.

I was building a universe where power corrupts, where control is exposed for what it is, and where the human heart — broken, brave, bruised — still rises.

Witchborn wasn't just a story.

It was a reclamation.

It was my childhood dream stepping into the world with me.

It was the first breath of a life that belonged entirely to me.

Becoming an author gave me a new sense of self.

After years of negativity, fighting, bracing, and darkness, the creativity was a much-needed balm.

It reconnected me to the part of myself I'd buried under survival — the imaginative, intuitive, powerful woman who had stories to tell.

Writing gave me something bright to look forward to.

CHAPTER 1

It gave me momentum.

It gave me a sense of belonging in a world I chose, not a world forced onto me.

Most of all, it made me the narrator again.

The director.

The architect of my own future.

***

The Life I Live Now

Today, I live my life — not his.

His passion for motorbikes became mine, I still ride.

I love the freedom, so it is on my terms.

But everything else has shifted.

My days are simple and intentional:

growing food in my garden

hiking

kayaking and biking

nourishing my body

working for myself

building my author business from the ground up

creating something that will outlive me

spending time with my family and friends, knowing how precious those hours truly are

choosing privacy, choosing peace, choosing myself

living as self-sufficiently as possible

treating myself with the love I once gave away too easily.

I am rebuilding a life that feels grounded, sacred, and entirely self-directed.

***

The Woman I See Now

When I look at myself now, I don't see damage.

I don't see scars.

UNBROKEN

I don't see a woman broken by the things she survived.
I see a woman carved by experience —
not hardened,
but evolved.
I see someone who has walked through fire and kept her softness.
Someone who has faced every demon with bare hands and refused to become one.
Someone who has outgrown her own mask.
Someone who has seen the architecture of her wounds and rebuilt herself anyway.
I see a woman who:
loves fiercely and deeply
is loyal in a world that has forgotten the meaning
protects her peace the way a mother lion protects her cubs
chooses radical self-trust
regulates her emotions with intention
owns her intuition
faces pain instead of running from it
integrates every lesson, no matter how brutal
refuses to dim her fire for anyone
I see a woman who has lived a thousand lives inside one lifetime —
and who is finally living the right one.
This chapter isn't about survival.
It's about expansion.
About identity.
About purpose.
About the woman I became when the noise of violence fell away and the truth of who I am finally had room to rise.
Thriving didn't happen by accident.
It happened because I chose myself — again and again — long after the world expected me to fall.

Reflection

"When a woman rebuilds her life, she does not return to who she was — she returns to who she was always meant to be."

Thriving isn't loud.

It doesn't announce itself with fireworks or declarations or turning points that feel cinematic.

Thriving is subtle — the steady return of self-respect, the quiet expansion of a life no longer shaped by fear, the calm knowing that the world inside you is finally yours again.

It is the moment you realise you're not rebuilding from what broke you — you're building from who you've become.

And that woman?

She's not a survivor trying to rise.

She's someone who already has.

VI

TRUTH-BOMBS

Chapter 1

"Even the strongest heart bends under the hand it trusts."

Ten Psychological Truths Every Survivor Should Know
   You didn't stay because you were weak.
   You stayed because your nervous system was hijacked.
   DV rewires the brain.
   Intermittent warmth + terror is the exact formula used in torture conditioning.
   It creates a trauma bond so strong it mimics addiction — chemically, neurologically, and emotionally.
   You didn't stay because you lacked strength.
   You stayed because your biology was working against you.
   And you survived anyway.

***

Love bombing is not love — it's manipulation in a pretty costume.
   Love bombing feels like connection, destiny, spark, "finally being chosen."
   But psychologically?
   It is attachment flooding — a tactic that overwhelms your system so you attach quickly, deeply, and before the real personality is revealed.
   If the beginning was "too much, too fast, too intense,"

it wasn't magic.
It was grooming.

***

Abuse always escalates.
Always!
There is no plateau.
No "this is as bad as it gets."
Abusers escalate in:
violence
emotional cruelty
control
cheating
psychological degradation.
It always gets worse.
Survivors who understand this fact leave earlier.
Survivors who don't are often the ones we lose.

***

Abusers don't change because you love them enough.
They change only when they choose to — and most won't.
DV science shows:
1–2% of abusers reform sustainably
ONLY with long-term trauma therapy
never because a partner "loves them right."
You didn't fail.
He didn't choose to grow.
Those are two different truths.

***

Abuse creates cognitive dissonance — you hold two realities at once.
You can love someone
and fear them.

CHAPTER 1

Want them
and know they'll kill you.
Miss them
and be relieved they're gone.
This is not "madness."
It's a survival adaptation.
Your brain was trying to keep you alive inside an impossible situation.

***

Shame is not proof of guilt — it's residue from being blamed for your own suffering.
Survivors often feel:
embarrassment
stupidity
guilt
disgust
self-hatred
None of that belongs to you.
Shame is a scar left by someone else's violence.
Once you name it, it loses its power.

***

Abuse changes your body, not just your mind.
Long-term DV causes:
adrenal exhaustion
insomnia
panic attacks
chronic pain
digestion issues
hormonal disruption
memory gaps
hypervigilance
Your body was in fight-or-flight for years.

Recovery is physical, not just emotional.

✱✱✱

Leaving isn't a moment — it's a strategy.
Most survivors leave:
7 to 12 times
over months or years
in small psychological exits before the physical one.
Every time you tried to leave was a step toward freedom.
Every attempt counted.

✱✱✱

Healing isn't pretty — it's grief, rage, clarity, and rebuilding self-trust one brick at a time.
Some days you feel powerful.
Some days you feel broken.
Some days you want him back.
Some days you want him dead.
All of it is normal.
All of it is part of healing.
There is no "right way" to come back to yourself.
There is only the way that keeps you alive.

✱✱✱

The woman you are becoming is not the woman he destroyed —

she's the woman who outlived him and outgrew every version of herself that ever tolerated him.
Healing isn't about forgetting.
It's about evolving into someone he never would have survived standing next to.
You're not "returning to who you were."
You're becoming who you were always meant to be.
A woman sharpened by truth.

CHAPTER 1

Armoured in self-trust.
Rooted in peace.
And unrecognisable to the version of you he tried to break.

Chapter 2

"Where understanding exists, a survivor rises.
Where pressure exists, she disappears."

What Survivors Really Need (But Are Rarely Given)
There is a long list of things people think survivors need.
Pep talks.
Platitudes.
Inspirational quotes slapped over pastel graphics.
A "you're so strong" as though validation alone rebuilds a life.
But the reality is far less glamorous and far more human.
Survivors don't need clichés.
We need space, safety, stability, and truth.
We need humanity that runs deeper than slogans.
And what we actually need almost never matches what the world assumes.

***

We Need Safety That Isn't Conditional
Leaving violence doesn't magically create safety.
It creates possibility — and possibility is fragile in the beginning.
What survivors need isn't:
someone to fix us
someone to rescue us

someone to tell us what to do
We need:
somewhere we can breathe without listening for footsteps
space to sit without bracing
a life where no one is monitoring our tone, expression, silence, or words
Safety is not a feeling at first.
It's a practice.
A slow rewiring.
A body remembering it no longer has to shrink.
Some days safety looks like sitting on the floor with a cup of tea and realising the room is quiet.
Some days it looks like sleeping through the night for the first time.
Some days it looks like trusting that the knock at the door is just a knock.
Survivors don't heal inside pressure.
We heal in safety.

***

We Need Permission to Be Human — Not Heroic
People love survivor stories because they want the triumph.
They want the comeback.
They want the phoenix rising from the ashes.
They forget that before a woman rises, she collapses.
What we need isn't hero-worship.
It's permission:
to be messy
to feel conflicted
to grieve
to be angry
to still miss the fantasy
to have days where progress looks like brushing our teeth

to say "this still hurts" without someone expecting immediate inspiration.

Healing is not linear, and it isn't pretty.

It's human.

And survivors need the space to be human without performing strength for anyone else's comfort.

***

We Need People Who Don't Turn Away from the Truth
The truth of domestic violence makes people uncomfortable.
It shatters illusions.
It forces them to confront the fragility of their own safety.
So, they look away.
They minimise.
They explain it back to you in ways that make them feel better.
What survivors need is the opposite:
people who can sit with the reality without flinching
people who don't sanitise the story
people who don't say "but he seemed so nice"
people who don't rush to judge what they've never lived
people who can hold truth without collapsing under it.
We don't need saviours.
We need witnesses — steady, grounded, compassionate witnesses — who allow our truth to exist without trying to edit it.

***

We Need Understanding Instead of Advice
Advice is easy.
Understanding is work.
Most advice given to survivors is well-intentioned and deeply unhelpful:
"Just don't go back."
"He's not worth it."

CHAPTER 2

"You're better than that."
"You should see a therapist."
"You're strong — you'll be fine."
None of those sentences address the body.
The trauma bond.
The psychological hooks.
The impact of isolation.
The damage done by coercion.
The way your nervous system lies to you.
The years of conditioning that shape your reactions long before a violent man enters your life.
Survivors don't need advice.
We need people who understand the architecture of trauma.
People who say:
"I hear you."
"I'm here."
"You're not crazy."
"What you feel makes sense."
"You don't have to explain why it was hard to leave."
"You are not alone."
Understanding builds healing.
Advice builds walls.

***

We Need Time — Real Time
Healing doesn't happen in weeks.
It doesn't happen on someone else's schedule.
It doesn't happen because the relationship ended.
The world loves quick resolutions.
Survivors need time:
to rewire our nervous systems
to re-learn what peace feels like

to rebuild trust in our own intuition
to understand patterns that took decades to form
to slowly shed the remnants of fear
to reconnect with our own identity unfused from the abuser
Time is not passive.
It's active rebuilding.
And survivors know better than anyone:
Time isn't the healer.
What you do with it is.

***

We Need Self-Trust More Than Anything Else

Before a survivor trusts another person again, she needs to trust herself.

Self-trust was the first casualty of the violence.

When someone manipulates your reality long enough, your instincts get cloudy.

Your internal signals get distorted.

Your intuition gets overridden by survival programming.

Rebuilding self-trust is not a mindset.

It's a process:
listening to your body
paying attention to discomfort
honouring the voice that whispers "something's off"
recognising early signs of danger
refusing to rationalise red flags
choosing your peace over your loneliness
believing your first reaction instead of talking yourself out of it
Survivors don't heal by trusting others again.
We heal by trusting ourselves again.

***

We Need a Future That Has Nothing to Do with Them

CHAPTER 2

The biggest shift in healing is the moment your future stops referencing your past.
When your plans aren't shaped by trauma.
When your dreams aren't rebounds from pain.
When your life isn't built in opposition to what happened — but in devotion to who you're becoming.
Survivors need:
purpose
passion
creativity
connection
independence
understanding
meaning
identity beyond survival
We need dreams that exist because we exist —
not because of what we lived through.
We need the freedom to rebuild a life that is ours.
A life where violence is not the reference point.
Where control has no foothold.
Where love is steady and grounded.
Where peace is normal.
Where purpose swells up from inside instead of being forced out in defence.
Most of all, we need the world to stop asking why we stayed —
and start asking how they can help women leave safely
and rebuild powerfully.
Here's the truth:
Survivors don't need permission to rise.
We need room to.
And once we have that room — we rise on our own.

Chapter 3

"A trauma bond ends the moment honesty becomes stronger than hope."

How to Recognise a Trauma Bond

You cannot break a trauma bond you cannot see.

And most women don't recognise the bond — not because we're naïve, but because trauma bonds disguise themselves as:

love
intensity
chemistry
destiny
"connection"

But at its core, a trauma bond is nothing mystical.

It's attachment formed under:

threat + inconsistency + fear + intermittent "love."

Here are the *real* markers DV psychologists look for — the red flags that define a trauma bond long before violence escalates.

***

You feel chemically hooked to him — even when he hurts you.

Intermittent reinforcement creates the same neurological loop as addiction.

You feel pulled back like a magnet you cannot shut off.

CHAPTER 3

Not love.
Biology.

***

You defend him — even when you know he's dangerous.
You protect the version of him you *wish* was real.
That's not devotion.
That's survival logic.

***

Your brain replays everything like it's studying for an exam.
Conversations.
Arguments.
Apologies.
Imagined futures.
Imagined reconciliations.
Imagined disappearances.
DV experts call this intrusive rumination — the brain trying to build predictability inside a relationship built on unpredictability.

***

You fear losing him — even though he terrifies you.
Your body remembers the consequences of upsetting him
just as your mind remembers the affection you're trying to hold onto.
This contradiction is the trauma bond.

***

The "good bits" feel supernaturally intense.
When sweetness is rare, the hit is stronger.
You're not experiencing love — you're experiencing withdrawal relief.

***

You blame yourself for *his* violence or cruelty.
You rewrite your own reality to feel safer:
"If I just didn't…"
"If I were calmer…"

"If I didn't trigger him…"
Conditioning, not truth.

***

You feel unsafe with him — but more unsafe without him.
This is the heart of the bond.
Your nervous system confuses "familiar danger" with "safety."

***

Your body reacts physically when you pull away.
Nausea.
Shaking.
Cravings.
Panic.
Insomnia.
Withdrawal symptoms identical to drug detox.
Because it is drug detox.

***

The relationship feels epic — even though it makes no sense.
Not soulmate-level intensity.
Just fear, anxiety, instability and intermittent affection masquerading as "deep connection."

***

Core Truth
If you recognise even two of these signs, you weren't in a love story.
You were trauma-bonded.
And trauma bonds aren't symbols of passion —
they're symptoms of captivity.
Now that you can see it,
you can break it.

Chapter 4

"Illusion is the glue of a trauma bond;
truth is the blade that cuts it."

How to Break a Trauma Bond (The Hard, Unpretty, Necessary Truth)

Trauma bonds do not end when the relationship ends.

They end when *you* dismantle the psychological, emotional, and chemical patterns that tied you to him.

This is not strength.

This is **honesty**.

Relentless, ruthless honesty.

Here's how I broke mine — without shortcuts, delusion, or self-soothing lies.

***

You Start by Telling Yourself the Truth — Not the Story You Lived In

Not the dream you clung to.

The truth about:

who he was

what he did

what you excused

what you lost

what he never was capable of being
Truth is the first cut in the cord.

***

Break the fantasy — the most addictive piece.
The fantasy keeps women hooked far longer than the man ever did.
You grieve the dream.
Not him.
Once the fantasy dies,
the bond begins to starve.

***

Starve the chemistry (no contact = detox).
No messages.
No social media checks.
No rereading old texts.
No mental conversations.
No "just seeing how he is."
This isn't emotional strength.
It's **chemical withdrawal**.
Your body needs to detox the cycle
like a substance.

***

Fill the empty space faster than the trauma can.
Trauma bonds survive in silence, stillness, and loneliness.
Structure.
Routine.
Purpose.
Nature.
Movement.
Creative focus.
Self-discipline.
Purpose is the antidote.

CHAPTER 4

***

Study your patterns — not his excuses.
Understanding *your* psychology is what collapses the bond.
It dissolves shame.
It ends self-blame.
It replaces confusion with clarity.
A trauma bond cannot survive in a woman who understands herself.

***

Stop worshipping your endurance.
Endurance is not love.
Endurance is not compatibility.
Endurance is not evidence he's "worth it."
Endurance is evidence you can survive —
but survival is not the same as living.
Respect your need for peace more than your ability to tolerate hell.

***

Face the lie you've been avoiding.
"He would never actually kill me"
is the lie that kills women.
When you finally see the risk
instead of the romance
the spell shatters.

***

Let the body make the final call.
The mind gets confused.
The heart gets manipulated.
But the body always knows.
Mine knew the day I hugged him
and felt nothing.
Your body will cut the last thread
when it's ready.

***

Break the bond every day — until it stays broken.
It's not a single decision.
It's repetition.
Choosing clarity over fantasy.
Reality over longing.
Peace over craving.
Self-trust over self-betrayal.
A trauma bond doesn't snap.
It erodes.

***

Final Truth
A trauma bond is a prison you mistake for destiny.
Breaking it is rebirth.
You don't go back to who you were.
You rise into who you were meant to be.
You don't just leave him.
You return to yourself.

Chapter 5

*"Shame is a shadow — it vanishes
the moment you turn toward it."*

What To Do When You Feel Shame

How to dismantle the emotion that traps more survivors than fear ever will.

Shame is the quiet killer in domestic violence.

It's the emotion that keeps women silent, stuck, and spiralling long after the bruises fade.

Shame stops us from asking for help, telling the truth, or even admitting to ourselves what we lived through.

Shame isn't a flaw.

It isn't weakness.

It isn't proof you "should have known better."

Shame is a trauma response — a psychological imprint from years of coercion, blame-shifting, and survival-mode decision-making.

And like every trauma response, it can be undone.

***

Name the Shame Out Loud

Shame thrives in secrecy.

The moment you name it, it loses power.

Not a full confession.

Not a breakdown.
Just a sentence:
"I feel ashamed because I stayed."
"I feel ashamed because I fought back."
"I feel ashamed because I loved him."
"I feel ashamed because I hid it from people."
Naming it separates you from the feeling.
Shame is not identity.
It's residue.

***

Reframe the Story: Shame Means You Survived
Women feel shame because they think:
"I should have left sooner."
"I should have known better."
"I should have been stronger."
Here is the psychological truth:
You didn't stay because you were weak.
You stayed because you were trying to survive.
Shame is the mind's attempt to make sense of behaviour that kept you alive.
Reframe it:
"I stayed because I was calculating."
"I stayed because leaving was dangerous."
"I stayed because I still hoped for change."
"I stayed because I had compassion."
That isn't weakness.
That's humanity.

***

Speak to Yourself the Way You Would Speak to Another Survivor
If another woman told you the same story you lived, you would never say:

CHAPTER 5

"How could you be so stupid?"
"Why didn't you leave?"
"You should've known."
You'd say:
"You did your best."
"I'm glad you survived."
"You didn't deserve any of it."
"I'm proud of you."
Why should you deserve anything less?
Your inner voice must become your ally, not your abuser.

✶✶✶

Anchor Yourself in Facts, Not Feelings
Feelings lie.
Trauma lies.
Shame lies harder than all of them.
When shame rises, anchor to truth:
✔ DV escalates over time
✔ The cycle rewires your brain
✔ Leaving is the most dangerous phase
✔ Trauma bonds distort judgement
✔ Abusers manipulate reality
✔ No one chooses abuse
✔ Survival responses are automatic
Facts break illusions.
Facts break shame.

✶✶✶

Interrupt Shame with Present-Moment Awareness
Shame drags you backward into "I should have known,"
but healing pulls you into now.
Use grounding techniques DV counsellors teach:
Put your feet on the floor

133

Place a hand on your chest
Say your name
Say where you are
Say what is true in this moment
Shame lives in the past.
Presence cuts its oxygen supply.

***

Rewrite the Narrative: Replace Shame with Personal Power
Shame says:
"I'm broken."
"I'm weak."
"I let this happen."
Personal power says:
"I survived."
"I changed my life."
"I made choices that kept me alive."
"I am rebuilding intentionally."
Every time you catch shame, swap it for self-leadership.
This reprograms the nervous system.

***

Remind Yourself: Shame Is a Conditioning, not a Truth
Abusers cultivate shame on purpose.
They use it to:
isolate you
confuse you
weaken you
make you dependent
keep you silent
make their behaviour look justified.
Shame is not organic.
It was planted.

Your job now is to uproot it.

***

Let Yourself Feel the Grief Under the Shame
Shame is often armour over grief.
When you peel it back, what you feel isn't shame at all —
it's sadness:
sadness for who you were
sadness for what you endured
sadness for the years you lost
sadness for the girl who didn't know love should never hurt.
Let the grief come.
Grief is healing.
Shame is blockage.

***

Replace "Why did I stay?" with "How did I survive?"
This is one of the most powerful cognitive reframes in DV recovery.
"Why did I stay?"
invites judgement.
"How did I survive?"
invites compassion, pride, understanding, strength.
The second question tells the truth.
The first is a wound.

***

Remember: Shame Is Proof You Still Care About Yourself
Shame feels awful.
But psychologically, it means this:
You still have a moral compass.
You still have empathy.
You still have self-awareness.
You still know what you deserved.
You still know it wasn't right.

Women who don't care, don't feel shame.
Your shame is not proof of failure.
It's proof of values, integrity, and self-respect trying to return.

***

The Truth you Leave this Section with
You don't heal shame by erasing the past.
You heal it by understanding the past in a new way.
Shame isn't a verdict.
It's an echo.
And once you stop letting it speak for you,
your real voice — the one you rebuilt piece by piece — finally steps forward.

Author's Note About the Following Resources

When I finally left, none of the support listed was available to me.
Not because these services didn't exist —
but because they were overwhelmed, underfunded, and carrying the impossible weight of too many women trying to survive at once.
I was placed on waitlists.
Months-long waitlists.
And like many women, I had to rebuild myself alone.
I say this not to discourage you, but to offer clarity:
If you reach out for help and the system cannot catch you immediately, it is not because you are unimportant.
It is not because your situation isn't serious.
It is not because you are invisible.
It is because the demand is enormous
and the support networks are stretched to breaking.
I include this resource list not because it saved me —
but because:
It might save someone else.
You deserve every option available.
You deserve a path — even if it's slow, crowded, and imperfect.
You should know what exists, even if access is delayed.
And because no woman should ever have to heal the way I did —
alone, guessing, surviving on instinct.

This is not a guarantee of immediate assistance.
It is a map —
of what exists,
what may be available,
and where you can start.
If you reach out and don't get help straight away, keep reaching.
Keep trying.
Keep choosing yourself.
You are not alone —
even when the system makes you feel like you are.

Resources

Australia
Emergency
000 — If you are in immediate danger.
24/7 Crisis Support
1800RESPECT – 1800 737 732
National Sexual Assault, Domestic & Family Violence Counselling Service
(Phone, online chat, resources)
Lifeline – 13 11 14
24/7 crisis support and suicide prevention
DVConnect (Qld)

- Womensline — 1800 811 811
- Mensline — 1800 600 636

Crisis counselling, refuge coordination, and safety support
Beyond Blue – 1300 224 636
Support for anxiety, depression, emotional overwhelm

***

New Zealand
Emergency
111
Domestic Violence Helplines
Shine – 0508 744 633

DV support, safe houses, and legal pathways
Women's Refuge – 0800 REFUGE (0800 733 843)
24/7 support, crisis accommodation, advocacy

***

United Kingdom
Emergency
999
Domestic Abuse Helplines
National Domestic Abuse Helpline – 0808 2000 247
Run by Refuge; 24/7 confidential support
Women's Aid – Live Chat
Trauma-informed real-time chat support

***

United States
Emergency
911
Domestic Violence Helplines
National Domestic Violence Hotline — 1-800-799-SAFE (7233)
Call, text "START" to 88788, or use online chat
Love is Respect — 1-866-331-9474
Support for young women, teens, and anyone unsure whether their relationship is abusive

***

International
UN Women: Ending Violence Against Women
Global resources, advocacy, country-by-country services
International Directory of Domestic Violence Agencies
Search worldwide DV shelters and support services

A Compassionate Note for Survivors

These services exist because none of this was ever your fault.
  You are not dramatic.
  You are not overreacting.
  You are not imagining it.
  You are not alone.
  Domestic violence is a pattern, not an incident.
  Leaving is a process, not a moment.
  Trained professionals can help you navigate the safety, psychology, and logistical realities no woman should ever have to face by herself.
  You deserve safety.
  You deserve support.
  You deserve a life that feels like yours.
  This is not the end of your story.
  This is where you begin again.
  Writing this was the last step of my healing.
  It is the closing of a door I will never walk through again.
  The fire didn't claim me — it revealed me.
  And like the phoenix, I rose.
  And so can you.

About the Author

C.M.N. Rogers is a NZ born author living in Australia, whose life has been shaped by resilience, intuition, and a fierce commitment to truth. After surviving a violent relationship and rebuilding her life from the inside out, she turned her healing process into a mission: to give language to experiences most women survive in silence.

Her memoir, *Unbroken*, is a raw and unfiltered account of the psychology of abuse, the aftermath no one talks about, and the profound rebirth that occurs when a woman finally chooses herself. She writes with emotional clarity, visceral honesty, and deep compassion for survivors still finding their way out of the dark.

When she isn't writing, she can be found hiking through nature, building her author business, creating the Bellarose Legacy fantasy series, or tending to her garden under the quiet Queensland sun. Her work — fiction and nonfiction — is rooted in empowerment, shadow work, intuition, and the belief that every woman holds the power to rise.

You can find her on Tiktok/Facebook/Instagram @cmnrogers.author.

Also by C.M.N. ROGERS

C.M.N. Rogers writes dark, emotionally rich urban fantasy grounded in legacy, power, and the fierce bonds of family. Her stories blend supernatural suspense, generational secrets, razor-edged humour, and deeply human characters navigating impossible choices. Her work explores what it means to inherit both trauma and strength—and what we're willing to burn to protect the people we love.

Witchborn: The Bellarose Legacy - Book I
https://books2read.com/cmnrogers
Some bloodlines are cursed. Some legacies bite back.

Seraphina Bellarose wants nothing more than a quiet life far from the magic she abandoned—until her mother is murdered and her dormant powers surge awake. Returning to the Crescent Enclave with her teenage twins, she's forced into a world of haunted estates, unruly magic, and a sarcastic demon she never meant to bind. As old enemies rise and long-buried secrets claw free, Seraphina must face the man she once loved, the monsters hunting her family, and the terrifying truth running in their blood.

Witchmarked: The Bellarose Legacy -Book II
https://books2read.com/cmnrogers
Coming early 2026!

Some destinies hunt you. Some drag you through time by the hair.

Zinnia Hart never wanted magic, destiny, or the kind of legacy that comes with a body count. But when the Veil tears her out of modern-day New Orleans and hurls her into 1695—straight into the witch trials—she becomes the one thing this century loves to burn.

With a far too attractive woodsman she shouldn't trust, an angel with the patience of a wasp, and a bloodline she didn't know existed, Zinnia must outrun hunters both mortal and monstrous while her powers spiral out of control. Meanwhile, her family and friends in the present are tearing open every magical rule to bring her back.

www.ingramcontent.com/pod-product-compliance
Lightning Source LLC
Chambersburg PA
CBHW012208090526
44583CB00023BA/2981